# STORMY WEATHER, YET I STAND

## BEVERLY SIMS

**First Edition - First Printing**

Copyright © 2014 by Beverly Sims; All rights reserved.

No part of this book may be reproduced, stored in retrieval systems or transmitted in any form, electronic, mechanical, or by other means, without prior written permission from the author or publisher.

ISBN: 978-1-56411-024-4

Published in the USA by:
CB Publishing & Design
P.O. Box 560431
Charlotte, NC 28213
704.649.3585
cbpublishing-design.com
info@cbpublishing-design.com

# Special Acknowledgments

First, I want to give God the praise and glory for keeping me and having his Grace and Mercy upon me and loving me even on the days that I did not love myself. Father, you always let me know and showed me that I shall live because you live within me I thank you for allowing me and showing me how to live and begin this new journey.

To my husband Rodney, I love you and thank you for being so patient, understanding, loving, and encouraging me to stand up and do what I believe in. Thank you for being the husband and the backbone that God has called you to be in my life. To my mother, Ethel, Mommy, without you I know that I would not be able to continue the journey that God has called me to do; you have been my strength, you have kept me grounded, and taught me how to keep my head up no matter what, and I love you.

To my children, to Tehron, Robert, and Stefanie, I thank God for the three of you each and every day. You are truly a blessing in my life, I want to take time out to say thank you for the days when I cried on your shoulders and couldn't talk to anyone or didn't know what to say. The three of you, even at a young age, would run into my arms and just hold me and always say, "Mommy it's going to be okay." My babies, I want you all to know that you were right, it's okay,

Mommy has made it.

Through all those long journeys and struggles, today, I still stand and I have found peace! I'm ready to tell the world that. I love you all.

To my sisters and younger brother, thank you for your support, and the love you all have shown through many of my storms. There were days, even in my secret time, you somehow would show up and pick my sprit up when I was down, and no one else was around. I love you all for your compassion showing me love at all times telling me, "Big Sis, it's going be alright. No matter what, we are there for you."

A special Thank you to my oldest brother Michael, even though you weren't there through all of my storms deep down in my heart I know you were always there for me in spirit. Thank you for always listening and always giving me the advice that only a big brother can give Love you.

To my brothers-in-laws Pastor Chris, and Reggie, I truly thank God for the two of you, you both were there when I had little hope in my life, yet you both came to me and said, "Sis, keep your head up. God has the right one waiting on you, just wait on the Lord and his word was so!"

To Mrs. Ingram Garrick-Robinson, "Thank you for standing by me, believing me, and encouraging me. If it had not been for you and your 'Women of Empowerment' meetings each month, teaching women like myself that it's okay to step out of the box, today I feel empowered and free, giving God the praise for using you to encourage other women like myself. You are a phenomenal woman of God and you were right, it did give greater later, love you girl."

To Dr. Charles Washington, "Thank you for

taking time out with me, listening and encouraging me to press forward, I give God the praise for you. Thank you for being such an obedient man of God. Today, I stand because of you and the words you gave. Today, I am free because of you, because of the words you gave me, 'YOU ARE NO LONGER A VICTIM.' Today, I have strength because of you helping me find myself, once again, I am a strong women and I stand. Today, because of you, I'm ready to tell the world my story. Thank you, Dr. Charles Washington, may the Lord continue to use you to bless others as you have been a blessing to me."

# Table of Contents

Special Acknowledgments ............................................. 3

Chapter 1: Pure and Innocent ....................................... 9

Chapter 2: Touch by another hand ............................. 17

Chapter 3: Why me ...................................................... 49

Chapter 4: How low will you go ................................. 71

Chapter 5: Money won't buy love .............................. 87

Chapter 6: Here we go again ...................................... 97

Chapter 7: Living on the edge .................................. 107

Chapter 8: Life's too short ......................................... 119

Chapter 9: A liar and a cheat .................................... 127

Epilogue ...................................................................... 155

# Chapter 1

# Pure and Innocent

Reba was eight years old when she began to help her mother take care of her sisters. Their mother always worked hard and while they lived in New York City, she always made sure that a babysitter was there to take care of her girls when she went off to work.

Reba had a godmother named Leatha, who she looked at as a true angel. Leatha would see her about three times a week and she spent a lot time with her and her sisters. Leatha took them places like the park, art museums, carnivals, and even swimming at the large community parks. She was the one to buy Reba her first record player, which played 45's and albums. Reba was so excited when her godmother bought an album by one of her favorite groups – the Jackson 5. Reba's favorite song was, "Got to be There," and she played it all day and night.

Never the selfish type, Reba always shared with her sisters. She played her albums, and had so much fun with her sisters, dancing and having a wonderful time. Leatha cornrolled her hair in all the latest styles and sometimes she even created her own style.

When Reba went to school, many of her

classmates would ask, "Who did your hair?"

"My godmother," she proudly replied. She loved her godmother very much; and seeing her as a big sister, she always felt special when she was around.

One day Leatha did not come to visit and even though her mother and sisters were there, Reba felt so alone. Her godmother always came around and spent extra time with her when she needed some me time. That one particular evening though, Leatha could not make it and Reba's mother had already made plans.

"Reba, I'm only going to be next door and I won't be gone long. I'll put your sisters in bed and if you need me you can tap on the window and I'll be right home." Her mother explained.

Reba felt safe but a little scared, since she didn't know what to expect.

She asked, "Okay Mom, you promise just next door?"

"Yes," her mother replied.

Reba's mom put all her sisters to bed, just as she said she would. Although Reba was smiling, inside she was feeling sad, lonely, and scared knowing that their mom was leaving them home alone.

Before she left, her mother said, "Reba do not open this door for anyone other than me. Do you understand?" she replied Yes mommy I do.

Reba put the locks on the door and the iron bar that stayed behind the door as well. Then she went over to the window where she could see the other people who were gathering at her mother's friend's house. They were laughing and she could even see some of them dancing.

"There she goes," Reba said, "I see our mother dancing."

Realizing that her mother had indeed told the truth made her feel a little more at ease. Nonetheless, Reba kept going back to the front door to look out through the peephole. Suddenly, she noticed a stranger coming up the stairs of her building. Reba thought to herself, *Who is this man? I've never seen him before?*

Watching through the peephole, she saw him go upstairs and then quickly come back down. At that point, Reba began to get scared. She would never forget him; he was tall and dark skinned, with a scar on his face.

Reba wondered what he was doing as he went to her neighbor, Ms. Brown's house. She watched him go inside, and then she noticed him exiting with things in his hands. Continuing to look through the peephole, she watched as he went back into the house, still taking things from Ms. Brown and all she could think was, *Where is Ms. Brown? She should be home.*

Reba was really scared now, and tears were running down her face. She reached for the iron bar to make sure it was still latched across the door. Then, quickly returning to the peephole, she saw the man coming toward her house.

*He's going to come and take some things from us too*, Reba thought.

She quickly covered the peephole, now only able to see his shadow at the bottom of the door. He took the doorknob and wiggled it. When he realized he couldn't get in, he went back to gather the things he took from Ms. Brown and proceeded down the stairs.

Reba quickly ran to the window; knocked on the neighbor's window and asked, "Can you please hurry and tell my mom to come to the window?"

"Reba, is everything okay?"

"No! Mommy, I just saw this man go into Ms. Brown's house and take things. Then he tried to come into our house. Can you please come home, I'm scared!"

Her mother came home and Reba told her everything she had seen.

"Well, Reba," she replied, "Ms. Brown never came for help."

"I'm telling you the truth. I saw him go in and take her things."

About an hour later, Ms. Brown came knocking on the door as hard as she could. "Regina, Regina, open the door, it's Ms. Brown, I've been robbed!"

She proceeded to tell Reba's mother everything that had been taken from her home.

She heard her mother say, "Reba told me what he looked like. She saw everything."

At this, Reba's mom became very worried. She came in the room and said, "Reba, you were right. That man did something terrible to Ms. Brown; he did steal from her. I told her what you saw and she's on her way to call the police now."

Reba was devastated and scared, wondering why he would do that. Her mom stayed home for quite some time after that night and she never went to another gathering.

A month had now passed and it was a hot summer day, as her dad was sitting in the living room watching a baseball game. On days like this, her mom and dad would often put the windows up to cool down the house. Most of the kids in New York City would hang out on the fire escapes, talking to one another and shooting the breeze.

As night fell, Reba's father closed the window, but he forgot to lock it. As they were asleep, Reba heard someone coming up the fire escape and noticed that it was more than one person talking. All of a sudden, she heard the window go up and was very afraid. She could hear them walking around her living room. She tried to scream out to her mom, but her voice was too low.

Reba started to cry very softly and prayed to God, "Please protect all of us. Don't let anything happen to our family."

She could hear the men coming toward her room and slowly covered her head. Then she closed her eyes in fear and eventually dozed off.

The next morning, Reba could hear her mother scream, "OH MY GOD, we've been robbed!"

Reba jumped up and said "Mommy, I heard them coming up the fire escape and I tried to call you as loud as I could, but I was too afraid they would hear me."

Her mom said softly to her, "Reba it's a good thing you didn't, honey, because they could've hurt us all."

The police came, fingerprinted everything in the house, and took her statement. A week later, the police came back and said that they had arrested the culprit. What Reba later realized was that it was someone who had been in her home before. The robber turned out to be the neighbor's son.

After they left, Reba still felt unsafe and she asked her mother, "Why can't we just move?"

"Reba, we will be doing that in time, my dear."

As time went on, Reba noticed that some of the other kids on the block were starting to move away. It wasn't long after that when her mother said to her, "Reba, we're getting ready to move."

Her heart was saddened when her mother said that they were moving at that very moment. She replied, "But Mommy, what about Leatha? I don't want to leave without seeing her."

Her mother knew that Reba's heart was broken because she would not be able to see her godmother before they left.

Reba cried aloud, "No, Mommy, I cannot leave without seeing her."

She knew that there was nothing she could do though; they moved that night. Traveling upstate to Spring Valley, New York, was one of the hardest journeys that she would ever have to deal with. Leaving her fairy godmother and angel, the one that she loved with all her heart was extremely hard for her. There was not a day that went by that Reba didn't think about her. She felt lost and disappointed that she no longer had a big sister that she could run to or talk with. Many nights, she cried herself to sleep thinking about her. Even though she had her family, as time went on, Reba grew up feeling alone. There was something different when they left New York City. She was afraid that she would never see her godmother again. It was at this very moment that she vowed to never stop searching until she found her fairy godmother again.

# Chapter 2

# Touch by another hand

After relocating to Spring Valley, New York, times were hard for Reba. She and her family moved in with their cousin Vera, who had two boys of her own. Jeffrey, who was the eldest of the two, was rarely home. However, the younger brother, James always seemed to be around. Living with her cousin and her sons was different for Reba and her siblings, and at times difficult, as Vera was not always kind to Reba.

Although Reba never understood why she didn't like her, she learned to stay out of her way as much as possible. During the times when Vera treated her unfairly, her younger sister Ann was there to comfort her and she loved Ann dearly. In Vera's eyes, Ann did no wrong and was always her favorite.

Although her two younger sisters were too young to understand what was going on, Reba watched closely so she could learn the signs of her mood swings and stay out of the way. The house they all lived in was a two-family house; Vera's home was on the right and her boyfriend's was on the left. Vera spent most of her time with her boyfriend and his three children. They all got along, played well, ate dinner together, and had wonderful times.

Reba's mom, Regina, found a job shortly after they relocated to the Valley. It was summer when they first moved there, so Reba watched out for her sisters while their mom went to work. She knew it was okay because now she considered all of the children next door as family. They were now considered cousins, so with them next door, they were never left alone.

Reba quickly made friends in her new neighborhood. She and her sisters would go down the block with the other kids and play all sorts of games. They enjoyed summer days filled with hide and go seek, kickball, and freeze tag. Playtime was wonderful; the only thing their mom required was they were inside before the street lights came on.

She was always there waiting on them for dinner and to get them ready for bed. Although she worked a lot, their mother was always there to comfort them too.

In the meantime, Reba's dad remained in New York City and worked to save so that they could eventually move into their own place again. She knew that eventually he would come and live with them and this gave her comfort.

One summer, Reba's mother decided that she was going to send her and her sister to summer camp. The camp was called Sonny Akers, it was a Christian camp, and Reba was excited to know that they were going somewhere different.

Once they arrived at the camp, Reba and her sister Ann were so excited to see so many children from different backgrounds. It was here that Reba learned how to swim. The week was filled with new experiences for both Reba and her sister Ann. They went hiking in the woods, which allowed them to see animals and nature, not normally found in the city. They also had learning activities and Bible studies to teach them about the Lord.

Reba met a young lady at camp who became her friend and everywhere Reba went, she would go too. Ann also made her own set of friends, who were closer to her age. The last night before they went back home, they had a big bonfire with everyone from camp. Reba's new friend came to her and said, "Tonight after the bonfire, I'm going to sleep with you."

Not thinking anything of it, Reba replied, "Sure, that sounds like it is going to be lots of fun."

Later that night, when everyone pulled out their sleeping bags and prepared for bed, Reba's new friend put hers nearby, as she had said she was going to do earlier. They all stayed up laughing and talking until it was time for lights out. Then the young lady said to Reba, "I'm going to sleep with you in your sleeping bag."

Reba thought nothing of it, so she said, "Okay, no problem," not knowing any better.

The young lady climbed into her sleeping bag and got a little close to Reba, which she did not understand. While she was so close to her, Reba noticed that the young lady was putting her hands on her legs. She didn't understand that either. *Why is she now putting her finger in my panties*, was the thought running through Reba's mind. This was the nastiest and most disgusting feeling she had ever felt in her life.

Pleading with her to stop, Reba asked, "Why are you doing this?" She couldn't wait for the morning to come so this nightmare would be over. Because she was so confused and ashamed, she never told this secret. Although she did not understand, when morning came, she and her sister went back home. She knew she could not tell her mother because she didn't understand why the young lady did this to her. Never understanding how a so-called friend could do this to her, she decided that this was a secret she would have to keep forever.

Never wanting to return to that camp again, as time went on, Reba went back to her normal life. She went back to playing and having fun with her real friends and enjoying the rest of the summer days.

One summer evening, Reba felt like something was different but she didn't quite know what it was, so she continued her day as usual. Later that evening, Vera had company next door and their mother, Regina, decided to join them. Reba and her siblings had access to both sides of the house, so that particular evening, she and her sisters decided they wanted to go next door and go upstairs and have fun with their cousins, while all the adults were downstairs having a party and having their own fun.

Reba and all the kids were having such a wonderful time until one of the cousins decided he wanted to jump up and down on the bed. After a few jumps, he missed the bed and hit the floor very hard. Reba, being the oldest, was so startled and shocked, the first thing she said was, "We're going to be in big trouble." She knew that her mother had left to go to the store to pick up a few more things that the adults had wanted but Vera had stayed behind. Reba could hear her coming angrily up the stairs. The music downstairs had stopped and she noticed how quiet the house had become. Vera came in the room and started yelling to the top of her lungs at Reba.

Her sister, Ann, became very angry as well, and responded, "Why are you yelling at my sister? It wasn't Reba. It was Justin. It was Justin jumping on the bed and he fell off the bed and hit the floor."

Vera did not want to hear that, she grabbed her belt and beat Reba all through the house, hitting her with the belt buckle. Before she could catch her breath, Reba was falling down the stairs, screaming and crying, but Vera continued to beat her. Reba was so embarrassed and hurt that all the adults saw how Vera was beating her. She cried, running next-door, promising herself that she would never go over there again and she never did.

Her sisters Ann, Deborah and Mya left with her and tried to comfort her. "Reba, when Mommy gets back, we are going to tell her everything that just happened, I promise we will tell," Ann said, trying to console her.

Ann held her older sister tight until their mother arrived home. Then Ann began to tell their mother everything that took place. Regina became very angry and had a talk with her cousin Vera.

Then she came back and told her children, "Don't worry, we won't be here too much longer." Each day, Regina went out to look for a place for them to live. One thing about her, she was never one to hold grudges or stay angry very long Reba found herself at peace knowing that her mother would be moving them soon.

One evening, Regina went out with some of her friends. Reba was not afraid because she knew that her mother never left them for long, besides she knew that Vera was just next door. Vera's oldest son, Jeffrey, had left to go off to the military, leaving James at home. James was the one that Reba had always looked up to as a big brother. One evening, while Reba and her sisters were in bed, James came to Reba and whispered, "Come to my room for a second."

She asked, "Why, what's wrong?"

"Just come here and be quiet," he said.

Reba trusted James with all her heart. Not wanting to wake her sisters, she went into his room as quite as she could. She just thought that he had something to tell her.

"Sit down," he said.

Reba did just that. She noticed that James was acting kind of strange but because he was a big brother, she didn't pay any mind. Then, before she knew it, he was climbing on top of her. "Stop, James. What are you doing?"

"Hush, Reba. You better not yell," he said.

Reba did not like what he was trying to do and she started crying. "James, no, what are you doing? Why are you trying to take off my panties? Cut it out or I will tell."

"If you tell anybody, I promise you, I will hurt you." Then, with all his might, James pulled her panties off and placed himself inside of her.

Reba wanted to scream from the pain and she felt so nasty, as he began to move on her. She did not understand why he was hurting her. She thought he loved her, he was supposed to be a big brother. *What is he doing? Please make him stop, God please,* was all she could think.

Finally, James stopped and climbed off of her. Reba was in so much pain, hurting, crying, and afraid at the same time. As she stood up, stuff was running down her leg. She quickly went into the bathroom and continued crying, trying to clean what looked like blood and white stuff from her most intimate parts. At the same time, still wondering why he did this to her, she scrubbed her body clean. "Why did he hurt me? I always helped him. I loved him; he was my brother. I hate him. I hate him." She cried out. Reba wanted to tell her mother, she wanted to tell her sister Ann too, but she was too afraid and once again ashamed. She did not want anyone to think that she had wanted him to do this.

This was yet another secret that Reba vowed to keep at such a young age. The next day, James looked at her as if nothing had ever happened. She never understood how he could act this way and she hated the sight of him from that day on.

Reba was relieved when her mother came to them and said that they were moving into their own home. The day they moved, Reba was the happiest her mother had seen since they moved from the city. "Reba, you're awfully happy," she said.

"Yes, Mom, you really don't know how happy I am that we are moving into our new home, just like we used have when we lived in the city."

Reba was now thirteen years old and was beginning to feel out of place. Having experienced so much at such a young age, she was always wondering who she was, and what was going to happen next. When she thought back to the pain that others had given her, she would ask, *Why me?* She started to feel different, almost as if she didn't belong. Questions began racing through her mind: *Why do people treat me the way they do? Is it because of the way I look? Many people are quick to judge my outside before seeing or getting to know my inner heart.* Reba would ask repeatedly, *Why do they hate me so? Dear Lord, who am I?*

In the late 70s, it wasn't always easy for parents. While her mom did the best she could with what she had, it wasn't easy being a single mom with four girls. Reba's dad, Bill, finally left the city and came home; all of her sisters and mother were glad to have him back. He was a lot of fun and always played games when they came home from school. He would sit at the kitchen table, waiting for them to get home, so they could play checkers, Trouble, or even Monopoly. Reba always enjoyed her dad and couldn't wait to get home to see him. In Reba's heart, he was her hero. However, living in a three-bedroom apartment, with one bathroom, four girls, and two parents was a mess. There were times when everyone had to go at the same time, which sometimes caused Reba and her sisters to wrestle to see who would go first. Their dad was always the calm one. He would sit in the green chair and watch them go at it, until he couldn't take it anymore, then he would say calmly, "Now, that don't make any sense. Only one can go at a time."

Can you imagine, two girls to each room? Reba, the eldest, and her sister Ann shared a room, while the two youngest, Deborah and Mya, shared a room. Growing up,

Reba and Ann weren't the best of friends, or sisters; they were more like cowboys and Indians, or Ike and Tina. Ann always thought that she was the oldest and would tell everything about Reba, and this led to countless days of war.

Once Reba and Ann had a horrible fight in the house, just because Reba asked her to move out of the way so she could finish sweeping the carpet, not many could afford a vacuum cleaner back in those days. Well, that was it, and the next thing you know, Reba, and Ann were boxing, rolling all over the floor, and tearing up the front room. One thing Ann loved to say was, "You shut up with your big boobs."

Reba hated that, because they were bigger than those of the other children her age. She would respond, "You shut up. You make me sick."

Then Ann would snap back, "Well then, go to the hospital."

Reba replied, "You go to the hospital."

Before you know it, POW, there they go again, back on the floor tussling. Ann was always the tough one. The very last time they ever rumbled in the front room, it wasn't a good sight. They broke their mother's coffee table, and boy, did they stop and look at each other; they became best friends quick!

Meanwhile, the two younger sisters, Deborah and Mya, were screaming because they just knew that Reba and Ann we're going to die. "Quick, let's stand the table back up before Mom gets home." Reba said, and put the pictures back in the center of the table.

Days passed by and their mom didn't notice a thing. She would sit in the front room and watch the television with the girls. Back then, the television had aluminum foil around the antenna, and yes, they had one of those two. Reba looked and stared at her mother just as she sat her coffee cup on the table. Ann and Reba looked at each other like, WE ARE DEAD. The table rocked a few times but it never fell... "Whew, we made it through," Ann whispered.

It wasn't until one Saturday morning, their mother woke up in a good mood, she yelled out in a sweet voice, "Y'all get up and ready for our Saturday morning cleaning. When you are finished, we're going to get out and perhaps even go to the Bronx Zoo."

She put on *Soul Train*, which was followed by *American Bandstand*, and she turned up the television, like she was at a party. Then, "Reba, Ann, Deborah, and Mya, y'all get in here."

The first thing that came into Reba's mind was, *Oh Lord, we are dead, and I'm the oldest.*

Then Regina said, "I want all the rooms cleaned and the bathroom too. Today, I'll clean the kitchen and living room."

When her mother said that she would clean the living room, Reba's eyes got bigger than a boomerang. "No, Mom," she said, "I will dust and clean the front room for you."

Her mother threw her hands on her hips and replied, "Did you hear what I just told you to do?"

"Yes, Mom," all of a sudden she is mumbling and walks off toward the kitchen, then her leg hit that table and down it went.

Reba and her sisters scattered like flies.

"All y'all, get your behinds back in here right now!" Their mother yelled, "Somebody is going to tell me who broke my table and I want an answer now."

Silent, they all stood in a straight line, from the oldest to the youngest, in that front room.

"So, no one's going to answer me." Regina questioned, looking up to the sky. Then she said, "Lord, I know that the Bible says thou shall not kill, but if these kids of mine don't tell me who broke my table, I am going to skin them alive."

Who's the first name she would call... "Reba, you're the oldest."

Reba figured that if she just looked at her like she was the crazy one; just maybe, she would send her to her room. Reba looked at Ann from the corner of her eye and she could see Ann's lips getting ready to open her big mouth, and the two little ones were just standing there looking crazy.

Guess Ann couldn't take the pressure any longer, "Mommy, Reba hit me first and then we started fighting."

"Mommy, that's not true." Reba defended, "I was cleaning the living room and asked her to move because I was sweeping the floor. She was in my face and we started fighting."

Reba knew that she was going to get it either way; she had always felt that because she was the oldest, she would always be the one to get in trouble for whatever they did.

Their mother's famous line was, "You're the oldest, and you should have told them not to do that."

*Lord, one day, she is going to learn that these brats*

*just don't listen to me.* Reba answered, "They love to say, 'YOU'RE NOT MY MAMA,' and I'm tired of getting into trouble for what they do... Reba, who opened the cookies... Reba, why didn't my kitchen get cleaned... Reba, get me some water... Man, when I get older, I am going to change my name to who or why." Reba muttered under her breath.

"I heard what you just said under your breath, say it again and I am going knock your behind out..."

*How did she know what I said underneath my breath*, Reba thought. *How did she do that!*

"What? What did you say?"

"Mom, I didn't say anything."

"Go to your room now. You think you're grown, talking back. Lord, don't let me kill this child of mine."

Meanwhile, back at the ranch, as soon as Reba walked in the room, here goes Ann, "Ha-ha, that's why you got in trouble and if you say one word to me, I am going to tell Mommy."

*Someday, I am going to choke my sister unconscious*, was Reba's first thought. There were times when she wanted to go out by herself, without her sisters. Of course, their mother was not having that, her famous line for that was always, "Take your sister Ann with you."

All Reba could think was, *Err not her!* Lord knows, she would tell everything she saw or heard. Who wants their sister to always tagalong, especially when you're the only one from the neighborhood who always had to bring your sister everywhere you went. To even get out of the house, she had to come along all the time.

Reba would run down the stairs and out the front door, as fast as she could, trying her best to lose her. Yet, somehow, that girl could run like lighting and always catch up with her. Then Reba would run until she was completely out of breath, but somehow, Ann would always still find her, and then would have the nerve to say, "Huh, you thought you could lose me!"

One day, Reba asked her mother if she could go on the block.

"Go," she said, "go ahead and take your sister too."

Ann looked at her with that crazy look and said, "You heard Mommy, take me with you."

Well, this day, Reba told Ann, "Never mind, I am not going. I am tired of taking you everywhere I go!" She waited until she went to the bathroom, because Reba knew that this would be her only break down the stairs. Then she went running full speed, looking back the whole time she was running. This time, she decided to go visit her friend Dee at her house. It felt good sitting out in her yard, laughing and talking.

Then, all of a sudden, just when she thought she had lost her sister, one of her friends said, "Hey, Reba, isn't that your sister looking crazy across the street!"

All she could say was, "Dang, this girl is like a rat, always finding me like a piece of cheese!"

One day, when Reba was out with the girls, they were sitting around and talking about the boys on the albums and what they looked like, who's your husband, who's your boyfriend, you know typical girl talk. They all thought that Michael Jackson was going be their husband and the father of their children. Reba loved Forster Silver from the group the Slivers, Forster was the one Reba was going to marry and have a house with children.

Of course, Ann was ease dropping, and the first word out of her mouth was, "I'm going to tell Mom, you talking about some boys." Of course, when she got home, she did just that. "Mommy, Reba was down the street saying how some boy going to marry her and they are going to have some babies."

"Reba, what do you know about some babies?" Her mother asked.

Reba said under her breath, "Oh boy, here we go."

What did Ann do? She stuck out her tongue and walked off. Reba gave her sister a look as if she thought, *If I could just choke her and get away with it, I would.* Reba always knew why her mother sent Ann with her, and that was because she knew that she would come back and tell her everything she saw, heard, or even thought she might have heard.

Years went by, and now it was time for Reba to go to junior high school, her first year, and it was the most exciting time. Finally alone, without her tattle-tale/tag-along sister, they are finally not in the same school. Reba got a break; *now she could finally look at boys without her mouth of a sister Ann going back and telling.*

On her first day in junior high school, she walked through the doors and noticed that everyone was looking different from her, they all had friends and were walking around talking, smiling. Her mother, in her own way, had kept them sheltered, having four children, they were in church all day some Sundays. Reba really didn't mind though, since there were some cute boys in their church, and she didn't mind looking at them.

Every Sunday morning, they would ride to Newark, New Jersey, which was about a forty-five minute drive each way, to attend Pastor Mack's church. He was such an awesome man of God, Reba and her family always felt that he was a man ahead of his time. Pastor Mack would always teach his members that God is true to his word; we have seen and watched the Lord's Words come to pass. One thing about their mother, she did not play when it came to church, her family was going, and that was that!

With Reba being the oldest girl, she was not the one to have her hanging out. "That is what's wrong with these young folks today, just fast," is what her mother always said. "There will be no babies coming in this house, and I will not change any diapers."

"Lord knows, if I have to hear that again." Reba would say, shaking her head. Now, standing in the hall of the school, when the first bell rang, she just stood there alone, noticing that a lot of the girls were dressed different from her. The boys were looking different in junior high school as well. Weeks went by and the other girls always wore nice pretty clothing, they were able to change shirts and pants every day. Although Reba always wore the same four tops and three pairs of pants, she knew in her heart that her mother was doing the best she could with all of them.

Reba stayed to herself during most of her first year

in junior high. In class, she would sit in the back and watch how all the most popular girls, as well as the others, would laugh and talk to one another and have a good time. Reba always wondered how the other girls' households must have been. *What were their parents like? Do they live in big fancy homes, do they ride the bus or have nice cars, and do they have siblings like I do?* For weeks, she thought and pondered those very questions. As time went on, she began to feel like it was time for her to stop thinking about other homes and be thankful for the one she had, knowing her parents were doing the best they could for her and her sisters, all while giving them unconditional love. "Maybe I need to change and try to make some friends," Reba said to herself.

As time went on in junior high, she did make friends. She was still not the most popular, but it was okay. At least she wasn't feeling so alone anymore. Finally, Reba's first year in junior high school has come to an end, and one particular Saturday there was a block party at the school, DJ music, and food. Reba's friends said they were going, "Reba, do you think your mom will let you come?"

She replied, "Yes of course," before she knew it fell out of her mouth. "Girl, please. My mom is cool; yea, she is going to let me come." Then, she thought to herself *Lord, how can I ask my mother can I go to this one.*

Everyone was talking about it all week at school. The morning of the block party, Reba got up early to do her house chores, as she cleaned the bathroom and wiped the mirror, she stopped, took a real good look at herself in the mirror, and said, "Girl, you don't look that bad. Why don't the popular girls pay me any attention? I have long hair, nice shape, and my teeth are not crooked. Anyway, I'll just keep making my own friends."

With the house finally clean, Reba noticed her sisters watching her every move. She didn't pay them any attention though because she was in a bubbly and cheerful mood, singing along with all the songs on *Soul Train,* "People of the World Join Hands," by the O-Jays was jam that Saturday morning.

"Well, here I go," Reba finally said. She was nervous; hands sweating, she took a deep breath and walked into her mom's room, prepared to ask if she could go to the block party. "Mom, do you have a minute?" She walked even further into her mother's room and sat on her bed. Then she said, "I cleaned the house."

"Yes, I know," her mom replied.

Out of the corner of her eyes, as Reba looked over at the door, whom did she see standing there but Ann, trying to hear and see what Reba was up to. "Mom, there's a block party at the school today and I was wondering if I can go?"

"Reba, what time does the block party start?"

"It starts at 12:00 noon!"

"You can, yes."

Then she shouted, "Mom, do I have to take Ann?"

"No, not this time. I trust you, just be back in this house no later than 4:00 pm."

Reba was so excited; she looked at Ann, threw her head up in the air, and said, "Not this time, sister."

Then she went in their room and grabbed some clothes, took her bath, and put on her Sassoon jeans and shirt, along with her Members Only jacket, and out the door she went.

    The mother of one of her friends gave them a ride, and as you know, her mom had to check that out! Reba kept looking over her shoulder, waiting for you know who (Ann) to peek around the tree or be ahead of her but she was not there. When they arrived at the school, a few of her friends were standing and waiting for them out front. The DJ was jamming and you could hear the music playing loud; it was packed with kids from other high schools. It was amazing, "my first party," Reba said to her friends.

    They were playing music from school that was on the radio… "Girl that's the jam," Reba's friend Dee said.

    "Mine too!" Reba and the other friends replied.

    One thing Reba knew that she could do and that was dance! Then her jam came on "Let's Dance to the Drummer Beat," by Herman Kelly. Everybody got off the walls, and went to the center of the floor to dance, including Reba. She was dancing with her crew. Then the next thing they noticed, guys from another school came over and began dancing with them. They were so excited and now Reba and her girls were really dancing to the drummer's beat… in Reba's mind she was saying to herself, *Ha-ha… Ann's not here to see me now.* Then she began to dance even more.

    Reba looked up to see which guy she was dancing with, she looked and lost the beat to the music, "OMG, he is fine," she said to herself. "Is he really dancing with me?"

    Reba looked around and noticed that other girls were looking and saying, "Who's that chick Braxton is dancing with!" The whole time, Reba and Braxton talked and danced. *He was really a nice guy*, Reba thought. When he was talking to Reba, in her mind she was saying *Sorry "MJ" and Foster Silver, I found my husband, and I am going to marry him.* Her thoughts were so loud; Reba didn't hear a thing he said! Nonetheless, she knew that it would be time to go soon and she had to tell him something to get away, even though she didn't want to. He was her first guy friend. All she could think of was, "Let me get over here with my girls."

He replied, "Hope to see you again, where do you live?"

*LORD, HAVE MERCY DID THIS BOY ASK ME WHERE DID I LIVE? OH, I KNOW HE IS TRYING TO GET ME KILLED!* But all she could say was, "Why? I don't live around here!"

You talk about walking off fast, she almost passed her friend, until Dee said, "Reba girl, slow down."

She could see him with his friends, standing there and talking to them, but keeping his eyes on her.

"Girl, who was that fine guy you were dancing with?"

"I don't know! But all I can tell you is his name is Braxton."

"Girl, don't look, but he is still staring over here!"

"Okay, so now y'all know I am acting cute," Reba replied, smiling back at him. He winked his eye, "Oh Lord, that boy winked his eye. Did y'all see that?"

"Yes, girl. We did. You go girl!"

Looking at the time, they all knew it was almost

time for them to go, and please believe that Reba and her crew were not ready to leave, especially seeing that more people were still coming and it was already after 3:30 pm.

When Reba asked what time they were leaving, they all answered simultaneously, "when it is over." Her heart dropped, Reba couldn't believe that their parents would let them stay.

"Reba, girl, what time are you leaving?"

Now it was almost 4:00 pm and Reba knew it was time to go, "Girl, I'm getting ready to go now," she answered. She knew that her mom did not play that, what she said is what she meant...

Reba's dad was sitting out front waiting on her in his big red Cadillac. She had to play it off, as she didn't want her friends to know that she had to be home by 4:00 pm. Therefore, she told them that she had to get home because her mom had to work and she has to watch her sisters.

Reba's dad was really the coolest though, he asked her if she had a good time and Reba told him, "Yes."

He said, "I can tell."

She looked at her dad with the biggest smile. A man of few words, he smiled back and kept on driving.

On the way home, she kept a smile on her face, thinking, *Wow I danced with a guy and he was so cute. He went to Kayak Junior High School; his name was Braxton, fine pretty soft hair, dark skin, slim, and a very nice smile. We talked and danced the whole time I was there. I can't believe it, he chose me and I am not popular.*

They finally made it home and her mom was in the

kitchen cooking dinner, "So, how was the party?"

"It was great! We had fun; there were a lot of people there. I wish I could have stayed longer though."

Regina simply said, "You will have plenty of time to party."

That didn't faze Reba one bit, what her mother just said, she was too busy holding on to what she did and whom she met. Even though she knew she would probably never see him again, the mere thought of Braxton kept a smile on Reba's face.

After making it through junior high, it was now time for senior high school. Many of Reba's friends would not be going to the same school, due to the school districts changing. Reba felt like, *Here I go again, new school and a new beginning.*

Now attending Spring Valley Senior High School (SVSH), she knew it was time to change her thoughts and daily patterns. One day, the bell rang and it was time to change class, as she watched the other girls walk around the halls of the school, she could see the football players checking them out, calling them "sexy" and saying "how hot" this one looks. There were guys leaning on the lockers rapping to the girls. She could hear them saying "What's up girl? What are you up to? What's up with you after school? Call me, here is my number..."

*Blah, blah,* is how Reba felt about all that. A few of the football players were in some of her classes though, so she decided to get to know them. A few of the cheerleaders were in her gym class too, but they always thought that they were better than everyone else was. Reba tried out once, but it just wasn't for her. She felt as if she didn't belong.

It amazed her how she would walk by the football team, hockey team, or even the basketball players and not one would say anything but "Hello" or "What's up" to her, just like she was another one of the guys on the team. Guess it was like that because Reba didn't have one of their jackets. She began to wonder if it was because of what she wore, or was it because she wasn't popular, or maybe it was because she didn't wear lip-gloss like the other girls. Reba even wondered if perhaps it was the way she wore her hair.

Each day, when she got home from school, she would go in that bathroom and look in the mirror. As tears rolled down her face, she would say to herself, "One day, I will have it going on, just like the other popular girls. I am going to have that pretty hairstyle and wear the nice clothes and then I will be sexy, hot, and sizzling. Then just maybe, then I will fit in."

Reba often wondered why she always felt alone. *Was it because she didn't have an older sibling to talk to? Or was it because the only true friend she ever knew and had has not been not in her life for quite some time, and that was her godmother, Leatha Brown, and now she was gone.*

When Reba and her family moved, they lost contact with her godmother. Now, thoughts of her godmother began racing through her mind once again. Reba had loved it when her godmother took her to the art carnival on Amsterdam Avenue, it was a place where kids could go and work on arts and crafts, make movies, and do so many neat things. It was actually a place to keep kids off the streets and out of trouble. Her godmother would do things with Reba that most of the young girls on her block in New York City wished they could do too.

For years, Reba wished she could see and find her again, and just tell her in her own voice how much she missed her and loved her. In her mind, Leatha was truly a fairy godmother and Reba needed her now more than ever before.

She could hear her mother calling, "Reba, come on in this kitchen, it's your turn to clean."

One evening, as she was standing at the sink washing the dishes, looking out the window, Reba began to daydream and say to herself, "One day, I'm going to have me a fancy car. I'm going to have a house. I'm going to have me three children, two boys and a girl, and a husband that will love me for me and I will be so pretty." There were times when she said these things because she didn't feel that way about her herself. Even though people would always say, "Reba, you are so pretty," or "Reba, you have long pretty hair," each time, someone told her that, she would run to the mirror and stare at herself. However, she could never see exactly what they would see!

Reba did notice one thing though and that was that her breasts were getting bigger and bigger, larger than most of the girls in school. Nonetheless, no one paid her any attention, so obviously it was not the boobs that the guys were looking at. By the end of her sophomore year, nothing had changed. She still wasn't the most popular girl and she had made very few friends. However, the friends she made were people with whom she could relate. It was the last day of school when she told herself, *When we return back to this school, I am going to be a whole new Ms. Reba, somehow, someway!* Indeed, she came up with a plan to be a brand-new person, with a brand new look.

When summer vacation hit, Reba found a job. She worked at a place called Letch Worth, which was like a day care for challenged people. Her goal was to do some things on her own for school next year and she did, which was the best thing that could have happened to Reba.

Each time she got paid, she would ask her mom if she could walk down the street to the store called Masters, where she would find some pretty stylish clothes. Even at a young age, Reba knew how to shop. Some days her mother took her to Caldors, which at that time was one of the biggest department stores. If she was lucky, she would ride the red and tan bus to the Nanuet Mall and rack up on the latest outfits, shoes, and sneakers. This year, she did it all on her own, "New style, new me." Reba said looking in the mirror, as she tried on her new clothes. Summer was now coming to an end and *Operation NEW REBA was now complete.* It was almost time to return back to school.

With classes starting in a week, Reba seemed happy but a little nervous as well. "Here we go, school is back," she said, as she rose up early that morning, so she could take her time in the bathroom. Looking in the mirror, having self-talk, "Reba, today is your day and you look good."

She brushed her long straight hair and put on her new blue pants, and her white blouse with ruffles going down the front. When she finished getting dressed, her only thought was, *Wow, I really feel so pretty and I don't care who doesn't feel what I feel today. Oh shoot, let me not forget my Vaseline to shine my lips.* Reba's mom didn't play that lipstick thing, besides Vaseline lasts longer than some old lipstick. *Who is going to know the difference?* She thought.

Senior high, eleventh grade, and finally she was starting to be noticed, not just by the girls but many of the guys too. Reba felt so good; now she began to walk the halls with her head held high. "Wow, after the change of my new look, I can really walk the hall with my head up high, not bothering a soul. This was great." Reba said to herself, "This is my year." She began to have a few more friends this year too, and all of the team players looked at her differently as well.

As Reba walked down the halls, she could hear people saying, "What's with Reba? She's looking good." There was one girl in the school who was the biggest and the tallest bully in the school and everyone was really scared of her. Laurie Johnson was her name, and boy, she was the bully of the school. She had a few other friends, but everyone knew they were her groupies and all wanted to be just like her.

One afternoon after the bell rang, Reba was walking down the hall trying to get to her next class, and Laurie was sitting in a cubby with her crew. As she got closer to the group, Reba could feel that something wasn't right. Although she knew that Laurie had never liked her, she never knew why. She was also aware that Laurie and her crew were watching her as she walked closer and closer. Reba knew that she had to walk pass them. As she got very close though, she kept her head up and acted as if she didn't see them. Reba was praying on the inside, *Lord just get me past these bully girls.*

Just as she was passing by, she heard Laurie call her out her name, saying "Look at this bit** with her light skinned hooker looking a$$, thinking she's all that this year."

All the students in the hall stopped to see what Reba's response was going to be. Reba was already tired of Laurie and her friends picking at her and always having something smart to say. So, on that day, at that very moment, she decided to stand up to Laurie, even though everyone at school was scared of her. Reba figured that if she can handle her rough sister Ann, she could handle Laurie. She stopped dead in her track, and backed up. The halls grew so quiet, you could hear a pen drop, and she said to Laurie, "What did you say?"

Laurie stood up, holding a Sugar Daddy lollipop in her mouth. Although Reba had to look up at her, she was already very angry, and she replied, "Say that again, Laurie. What did you just say?"

Laurie retorted, "I SAID YOU A BI*^CH and your mama is one too."

Reba lost her mind. Inside, she roared like a lion, and she was about to give little Miss Laurie all the years of built up anger she had inside. Reba knew that Laurie was about to get a fresh can of a$$ whipping in her life, something her mama probably should've done a long time ago. Reba balled her fist so hard and punched the day lights out of Laurie. Her candy went one way and her big behind went another. Not giving her a chance to get up, Reba was immediately on top of her, beating her down, as if she stole something. Reba was out of control, yelling, "I'm tired of you messing with me."

Reba had a break down moment and then she had a flashback of her sister. Then she felt someone pulling her off Laurie, as if she were some kind of wild woman. Half of Laurie's hair was in Reba's hands. Laurie's eyes were red and her lip was bleeding. It took two principals to pull Reba off of her and one of them got pushed on the floor in the effort.

*OH LORD, I AM DEAD!* Reba thought... *Did I really just push the principal on the floor! Lord, I hope they call my daddy.* But it was too late, when she looked down the hall, all she could say was, "Lord here comes my mother!" Both sets of parents, Reba and Laurie's, went into the principal's office. Reba was suspended for three days.

Her mother did not actually kill her, as she thought she would, but she had to listen to her all the way home. "Reba how many times have I told you, sticks and stones may break your bones but names will never hurt you? You can't go around fighting people because they talk about your mother!"

Reba thought her mother was crazy. *If anyone talks about my mama again, I am going upside their head again.* When she got home, Reba couldn't wait to tell her dad. He was the coolest.

They waited until Regina went in the other room, "Did you whoop that girl's behind?" He asked.

All she could say was, "Yes, I sure did."

He said, "That's what I'm talking about, you don't let no one bully you around, Reba. I know you're not one to go around and pick on people, but you always stand your ground."

Reba could remember, as a little girl, what her dad would always say, "You don't let nobody beat on you, if you do, you will have to answer to me."

*Was this the dad I knew who said very little words?* Reba thought to herself. She knew he wasn't playing and she sure didn't want to have to answer to him. The funny thing is, when her mom would come into the room, with her hand on her hips, her dad would act as if he didn't say a word. He would just keep on watching his baseball game.

When Reba returned to school, she was real popular. Everybody was coming up to her saying, "Girl, you put a whooping on that girl. She's not coming back she got kicked out of this school."

It felt good to be popular but Reba really didn't want to be popular because of that.

*Things have finally calmed down in school and gone back to normal and I am back on track*, Reba thought. This year, I can see and feel changes in me. As she looked in the mirror, getting dressed one morning, Reba noticed her hairstyle, she had been fixing it all kinds of ways. She felt good looking at her hair, until she looked down at her body. Reba's thoughts had now changed. *My breasts have gotten bigger. My stomach is flat.* As she turned to look round, *Oh my, I got a booty that is poking out.* Reba turned back and looked in the mirror and said to herself, "My goodness, I have a shape. Now I'm going to call myself Ms. Brick House 36-24-36, yes at the age of 16. Bam!" This is Reba's true measurement, *Oh my look at the time, it's time for me to step out this house and off to school.*

When Reba stepped off the bus and in the doors of the school, she had her hair done, pinned up, long bangs, and rocking another new outfit she had bought. From the corner of her eyes, she noticed that someone was looking at her. Talking to a few of her girls, one of them said, "Reba, here he comes one of the smoothest and coolest guys on the football team. He's always a good friend."

"Hey, Reba, looking good girl."

"Thanks, Barnard."

As she started walking down the hall headed toward her class, all Reba could say to herself was, "Wow guess the outfit and the slight heels, new doo, and the slight makeup was the answer." Now, you know that's what you call sneaking clothing out of the house in your book bag and when you get to school, you go straight into the girls' bathroom and change. If Reba's mother knew she had on eye shadow or a shirt cut low that Reba got from one of her friend's house…well the rest is history, you already know that. Reba had on plenty of Vaseline, because she wanted her lips to shine, she wore half a jar. Looking at the clock in class, it's time for the bell to ring.

As she was walking down the hall, Reba noticed

that a group of football players were huddled by the lockers in the hall. Inside, she felt herself becoming nervous; she felt them watching her, and they were staring at her in disbelief. Reba heard one of the players saying, "Is that Reba, she is looking fly," and others were now saying, "Yeah, the girl is real hot this year."

One of the players in particular really turned his head and watched her as she walked down the hall, and he was fine. He was one of the star football players in the high school and almost all of the girls had a crush on him.

Reba was finally feeling that she was fitting in and this was truly her year to shine. Most of the last year, the pretty fly girls would look Reba up and down as they passed her in the halls. One of the leaders of the pack had the nerve to say, "Who's this girl in school this year, 'bout time she got some new clothes, 'bout time she got a new hairdo. Now, she thinks she's all that and a bag of chips."

Ms. Fly Girl Chrystal, the pack leader, oh she was never one to approach Reba, even though Reba waited many days for her to do just that. She always had something smart to say each time she passed her. Nonetheless, Reba felt that it was cool; as long as she didn't step in her face, she could talk all she wants. Therefore, the more she made her smart comments about Reba, the more she would lift her head up. However, it came to the point that Reba felt like she'd give them something to talk about, so she began to put on a show for them, switching her behind and poking her big boobs out, slinging her long hair and smiling at the football players.

There were days when those same guys leaning on the lockers rapping to those so called pretty girls would now be walking Reba to her class, and now Reba is looking at those same girls saying to herself "and **what**!" She felt so good knowing that now she was somebody and she too was her own fly girl.

For the longest, Reba had wanted to fit in and feel like she was a part of something. One thing her mother Regina would always say was, "Good things come to those who wait," and she was right. Good things were starting to happen in Reba's life.

# Chapter 3

# Why me

Senior year is finally here and Reba felt more mature than ever. She had a hot shape, long hair, and was doing her own thing; Reba was feeling good about herself and her self-esteem was up. Once again, working over the summer and shopping for herself really paid off. New hairdo, smelling good, and she even wore some high heel shoes to school. Feeling like the new kid on the block, she was ready to face her final year of high school. Now, also dating one of the football star players, she was finally part of the in-crowd. Oh, the looks Reba would get, there were a whole lot of jealous girls looking at her saying, "Look at Ms. Thang, with the football jacket number 21."

Reba's boyfriend was fine and had it going on. He could tell Reba anything and she felt so good inside, especially when he would call her Miss Lady. Braxton always told Reba how sexy she looked and the other guys would look at him as if my boy got it going on. Time went on and Reba fell in love with Braxton, his nickname was "The Hawk"; he was tall, dark, had the juiciest lips, a shape like a body builder, and you could tell he was on the football team. Even with all of Braxton's popularity, he was still very quiet and laid back.

Reba was now starting to learn a little more about herself as well. She was discovering the young woman within her. "I am having feelings," she said to herself, "something different in my heart," and she knew she wanted to be with him forever. Reba always had a wonderful time with him.

Braxton finally asked Reba out to go to the movies. She didn't know what to say, the first thought she had was, *OH LORD, what am I going to tell or ask my mother.* Since Reba knew her mother was very strict, she decided to tell her that a few of her girlfriends were all going to take the bus to the Nanuet Mall to see a movie.

Regina looked at her with hesitation, but said, "Okay, Reba, I'm going to trust you be back in this house as soon as that movie is over."

She was so excited; she assured her mother that she would be home as soon as the movie was over. The next day Reba told Braxton that the movies sounded great, finally their first real date. They saw a Bruce Lee Roy film, they rode the red and tan line to the movies, and then they rode the same bus all the way home.

They sat in the back of the bus, holding hands, Reba resting her head on his shoulder, and then it happened, her very first kiss. When his lips touched hers, underneath, she could feel heat run down her body. *It felt so good, I am no longer that little girl,* Reba thought to herself. *OMG his juicy lips and sexy built body his arms has cuts in them from working out at all practice. What am I getting myself into?*

Since Braxton and Reba got out of the movies a

little early, he invited her to come over to his house. Because she felt safe with him, she decided that she would go. However, deep down inside, she had to be mindful of the time and make sure that she was home before it got too late.

As they entered Braxton's home, she was amazed at how nice it was. She met his mother; she was kind, very soft-spoken, and very gentle. She welcomed Reba into her home, looked at Braxton, and said, "Son, she's a good girl, you be nice to her."

Braxton replied, "Yes ma'am, I will."

After sitting in the kitchen with his mom for a while, Braxton invited Reba to come up to his room. Reba was very nervous about going to his room, knowing his mother was downstairs cooking in the kitchen; but Braxton looked at his mother and said, "Mom, is it okay for Reba to come into my room?"

She said, "Yes, Braxton that will be fine."

So upstairs Reba and Braxton went.

Reba was still nervous. As she sat on his bed, Braxton turned the television on and they just relaxed at first. Then something started to happen, Braxton got up and pushed his door closed.

Reba replied, "Braxton, why are you closing that door?"

He replied and said, "It's okay, my mom is cool with that." Braxton came back over and sat next to Reba.

He began to kiss her and Reba was feeling and saying to herself, "What is he doing? Why is he laying me down?"

Braxton called Reba's name in an odd way. Then

he started to whisper in her ear saying, "You know you are my girl; we have been together for six months now and I want you to be my lady. I want you to wear my football jacket to let everyone know that you are mine."

Her heart began to race, and then he whispered in her ears once again, "In order for you to be my lady, I have to have all of you."

Reba's heart began racing even faster, as he began to touch her in places that she didn't want to be touched. She was not at all comfortable with what was about to take place. It brought back thoughts of her past and the nasty feelings she had before. Reba yelled, "Braxton no, please I don't want to do this."

But he wouldn't listen; he was determined to take all of her, and he did. It was getting late and Reba was ashamed to leave his room, knowing that his mother was in her room. As they were leaving, Braxton knocked on his mother's door saying that he was getting ready to walk her home.

His mother answered, "Reba, nice meeting you. See you next time."

Reba responded, "Yes ma'am, and thank you."

Braxton and Reba were walking in silence. She had nothing to talk about; she was angry and felt so disgraceful, once again. Braxton grabbed her hand as if nothing had happened. He tried to talk to her, saying, "You're now mine, and I want you to wear my football jacket to school."

That was the last thing on her mind. She was still trying to figure out what happened and how did she let this happen to her. Lost and confused, this also felt very different from all the other unwanted abuse and touches.

Braxton stopped, put his hands around her waist, and said, "Reba, I do love you and I want to be with you for the rest of my life."

She had tears rolling down her eyes, because deep down inside, she was feeling the same way. She felt that maybe his love was true. Braxton and Reba's relationship grew stronger and she gave in because she loved him, and then she started to let her guard down.

After that, there were plenty of days when they would sneak off, go to his house, and just relax and chill, watch TV or even listen to a little "Fire and Desire," by Rick James.

As time went on, she noticed that Braxton started to change; he was becoming very jealous, not wanting her to talk to any other males at all! One day, he saw her in the hall talking to one of her friends, a guy, and Braxton immediately came up to her and just stood there. Everybody knew he was not happy, Braxton grabbed Reba's arm and said, "She will talk to you later!"

Reba was shocked and knew something wasn't right, "Braxton, why are you holding my arm so tight?"

He never said a word, but continued to pull her down the hall, and out the door, pulling her down the stairs. No one was in that hall but the two of them and he was in Reba's face, angry.

Reba could see the veins popping out of his forehead as he pointed in her face, "Didn't I tell you about looking up in other men's faces?"

Reba was so scared, she began to cry, trying to

explain, but he didn't want to hear it. He slapped her across her face and said, "If I ever catch you looking in another guy's face, if you think this slap hurt, you're going to get more than this."

Reba was so hurt, so devastated. Her parents had never hit her in this way, never talked to her in this way, and she was too scared to tell anyone what he just did. She wiped her face.

"Now go to your class and don't let me catch you again."

Reba went to class. She sat in the back, so quiet, so different, not feeling good. She just wanted to run home to her parents. This was the first beating of many to come. She had become so afraid of Braxton; she didn't know how to break up with him. He was so out of control, Reba knew that she wanted to share this with someone, but he always threatened her, "If you tell anyone, I will beat you dead," and because of the beatings that she had already been taking from him, Reba believed him.

Reba took Braxton's threats very seriously. If he thought she was looking at another guy in class, my goodness, Reba knew that he was going to beat her again. Reba even went to people that she thought were her friends and would tell them what she was going on, but their standard response was, "Reba, you are a liar, a liar he wouldn't do that, he wouldn't hit you… he's not even like that… girl, please, Reba, please… we have known Braxton since the second grade."

Reba was devastated and she knew after that that she could not share this with anyone else. She begged her

## My Life Story

friends never to repeat what she just told them. Their reply was always, "I won't, Reba, as long as you don't say that to anyone else and talk bad about our friend."

Reba dropped her head and said, "I won't." She was so hurt; she couldn't believe that friends she had known for years didn't believe her. Reba felt that if her friends didn't believe her, no one else would either.

Each day, she would go home after school and put on her happy face on in front of her family; but inside, she was so broken, her spirit, and her soul became more and more depressed. She would be so down that it didn't even matter what her sister Ann or the other siblings would say or do to her.

Many nights, she cried in her sleep, just thinking of what he said, and how he beat her, and she couldn't tell a soul. Because she knew that she would have to face the guy that she had once fell in love with, Reba hated going to school. Each day in class, she would sit far back and away from all the guys in the class, praying that none of them would come to say anything to her.

Then one particular day, Floyd, one of the guys who was friends with Braxton, came and sat next to her. He was talking to her, but she was trembling inside, afraid, she was saying to herself, "Please go away, don't sit next to me. You don't know, if he catches me, he's going to beat me."

Floyd was looking at Reba strange; he knew something was wrong with her. "Reba," he asked, "why are you so down? What happened to the bubbly Reba that I used to know?"

As she held her head up to get ready to answer

55

Floyd, she looked toward the door and there stood Braxton, staring at her with the most evil look she'd ever seen. All she could do was drop her head, as tears fell down her face. Reba already knew the sign that she was in trouble as soon as the bell rings. Floyd knew immediately that something wasn't right. He looked at the door and saw Braxton but he never said a word.

When the bell rang, Braxton was standing at the door of the class. Floyd walked out before her and gave him a dirty look. Braxton paid that no mind, he only had one thing on his mind, and that was Reba.

When she came out the door, she was shaking and looking around. She had nowhere to hide. Braxton looked at her with that evil look and said, "You will come with me and you will come with me now!"

Because Reba was so afraid of him, she begged, "Please don't beat me, please don't beat me, Braxton!"

Down the hall in a back staircase, he said with his hands around her throat, "Didn't I tell you about looking in other guy's faces?"

He slapped her continuously until one of the teachers heard the ruckus and yelling in the staircase. Ms. Wilson came through the doors and said, "Braxton you better not hit this young lady again. Reba come up the stairs right now and come into my classroom. Braxton go somewhere now before I get the principal and tell him exactly what I just witnessed and have your behind arrested!"

Mrs. Wilson went in the class with her and closed the door. She sat down with Reba, gave her some tissue and asked, "Reba, how long has this been going on?"

Reba was too afraid to talk but she was tired and worn out from his never-ending threats. She wanted so much to tell her family but she was scared that he would try to kill them too. There was so much Reba had been through with Braxton, he would drag her to his home and would have all kinds of awful sex with her, making her do things she didn't want to do. Reba cried and couldn't understand why was he so evil to her why would he make her do these things, when she never did anything wrong but try to love him. Reba began to wonder, *Why does love hurt like this? Why are the ones I love so always hurting me? Why did they beat me? Why did they step all over me? Why God, why do the people treat me like this?*

There came a point when Reba realized that her cycle did not come and she was so afraid, she couldn't tell her mother, and she couldn't tell any of her friends, because she realized that at the end of the day, she felt like she had no one but herself.

There was Sandra the one young lady that Reba thought was her friend, and she felt like she probably could trust her at the time. Sandra was dating Braxton's cousin. She had told Reba secrets as well, but Reba never shared those with anyone. She went to Sandra but never told her about the beatings because trying to share that with her other friends didn't turn out so well. Reba felt like no one would believe her anyway but she wanted to share with Sandra that she was pregnant by Braxton. She asked Sandra to never tell anyone until she figured out how she could tell Braxton.

Reba was now three months pregnant and still

hadn't told Braxton about her pregnancy, when he told her to come to his house. She was very nervous each time she went to his house. It was never a good ending but she knew that if she didn't go, he would find her. When Reba got to Braxton's house, she noticed that no one was home but him and she could see the look in his eyes. She knew immediately that she was in danger once again. Braxton yanked her in the house; then he pushed her on the chair and came close to her face, "What the hell is this? I hear you're pregnant!"

Reba dropped her head and began to cry out loud, "I'm sorry, Braxton, I'm sorry."

He snatched her out of the chair and slapped her so hard, she fell on the floor, curled in a ball, and just cried. Then he grabbed her by her hair and dragged her upstairs to his room; he beat her, punching her with his fists repeatedly.

Reba screamed, "Please stop, my eyes, I can't see, Braxton."

There was blood all over the place; then he began stomping Reba in her stomach. She was now screaming at the top of her lungs, "Stop, please stop, my baby."

Braxton yelled, "You will not have this child. You will not stop me from going to college. You will not stop my career." Then he grabbed her hair, began to pull it out, and stomped all over her stomach again, saying, "This baby will come out. I'm not having no baby, don't you know I won't be able to go to college! I won't be able to do anything that I want to do!"

The pain was so horrific, Reba passed out, not remembering much of anything. When she opened her eyes, Braxton was standing over her saying, "Reba, I'm sorry."

*My Life Story*

However, it was too late, when she looked in the mirror and saw her face, her heart stopped! The first thing that came to her mind as she grabbed her stomach was, *Lord, please be with me and my baby. Let my baby be alive, help me Father to get out of this house!*

Braxton stared at her with sorrow but it was too late. Reba hated him and the only thing on her mind was how, *I can't tell my mother, I can't tell my father, and I'm sure not going to tell my sister Ann.* She already hated Braxton because she knew he was doing something wrong to her sister.

He tried to put ice on her face and eyes. He knew that Reba didn't even look like herself. He also knew that she had to go home and he tried to think of every excuse to tell her parents, as to what happened to her face. He even tried to convince Reba to tell her mom and dad that they were playing football and the ball slipped in her hands and hit her in the face.

Braxton found a pair of his mother's wide faced sunshades and put those on Reba's face, even though they covered some of her eyes, they still didn't cover the swelling of her lips or the blood from her nose.

Reba looked in the mirror before she left Braxton's house and she cried even more. Her eyes were bloody on the inside and she could barely see. As she walked home alone, she prayed, "Lord please help me through this all. I'm afraid and I don't know what to do anymore. I know I have to go home to face my parents and my family. Please don't let them be angry at me, please."

As Reba entered her home, her mother was in the living room watching television and her father was laying down resting. Her siblings were in their room doing whatever it was they do. Reba tried to come in the house as quickly as she could, trying to bypass her mom, but her mother immediately knew something was wrong.

"Reba, get back in here right now."

Reba dropped her head and walked slowly into the living room. "Yes, Mom," she replied softly.

"Why are you wearing those shades this time of evening? Reba, take those shades off."

She slowly took the shades off her eyes. Her mother was shocked and devastated, looking at Reba with her hand to her mouth, tears fell from her mother's eyes, and she yelled, "Reba, who did this to you?"

Reba fell down by her mother's legs and told her that Braxton had been beating her for a very long time but she was too afraid to tell it because he threatened that he would kill her whole family.

Her father heard Reba crying and came into the room; he took one good look at Reba and became very angry. She had never seen her father look like this before, even her sister Ann became angry. One thing about Reba and her sister, they might fight amongst each other but they always had each other's back. Reba's mother just held her, as her father became increasingly angry.

Regina said, "Reba give me Braxton's phone number right now. I'm going to call his mother and let her know that we will be pressing charges against him."

Reba was so afraid, because at that time, all she

could hear was Braxton words, *If I ever find out you told your parents or anyone else, I will kill you all dead.* Tears began to run down her eyes. Her sister Ann comforted her and said, "Sis, it's going to be okay, I promise."

Reba could hear the phone ring from the other side, her dad sitting in his favorite green chair; she could see his face full of anger. The phone stopped ringing, "Hello Karen, this is Regina, Reba's mother."

"Oh, how are you doing?" Karen replied.

"Not good, right now I am standing here looking at my child's eyes and face."

"Well, what happened?"

"Braxton is what happened. He beat my daughter and I want to know why? Why in the world would he beat my daughter like an animal?"

All Reba could hear was, "Now wait one minute, she had to have done something to Braxton to make him act that way!"

Reba began to cry even harder because deep inside, she knew that no one would believe her again. Her soul was broken; she had tried to tell her friends, now his mother, and none of them believed her.

*Why,* is all that was running through her mind, *why?*

"Karen, I will be pressing charges against Braxton, and if he ever comes near my child again, I will make sure that he goes to prison!" Regina hung her phone up very hard, "I can't believe her, protecting him instead of finding out what happened. That's what's wrong with him now."

Reba's mother was beyond angry and her father paced the floors. Her mother had to stop him from going to look for him. "He's a punk, any man hits on a woman is a punk," her father said. "If he wants to hit on somebody, let him try to hit on me... Regina I pray that boy don't cross my path!"

Reba had so much going through her mind. She was worried about her unborn child that was beaten as well, she could barely see out of her eyes, and her mom wanted to take her to the ER but Reba was too afraid for that too, "No Mom, I'll be okay."

"OMG, he even pulled a patch of your hair out. Reba," her mother yelled, "he is just a damn animal!"

Reba laid down, and her mother and sister kept ice on her eyes throughout the night. She didn't sleep much though. She was too afraid. Every time she thought that she heard someone outside, she would jump up and peep out the window, but she saw nothing. It was an extremely long night.

The next morning, everyone in the house got upset every single time they looked at Reba. Days had passed, it was Saturday morning, and Reba decided to get some fresh air and go downstairs to check their mail. She opened the box and pulled all the mail out but she noticed that there was a little purple letter stuffed at the bottom.

Reba hesitated to pull it out of the box but she did. She noticed that it was addressed to her.

TO: REBA – FROM: BRAXTON

As she opened it, Reba began shaking and started feeling weak. There it was; the letter that she was so afraid of.

"Reba, so you had to open your mouth and tell

everybody, including my mother, just like you to do the opposite of what I tell you to do. You will pay for this. Don't you know, I could have set you and your whole family on fire last night while you were sleeping? I promise you will pay and you better get rid of that baby."

Reba was frozen, she was looking around to see if he was standing there watching her. Then she ran up the stairs as fast as she could, still shaking.

Her father was sitting in his chair, "Reba, come here, what's wrong?"

"Nothing."

"Reba, tell me. I know something is not right."

"No, Dad. I am okay." Reba gave her dad the mail and went to her room, putting her face in her pillow, *GOD why me? Why me?* Feeling so lost and lonely, she felt like she had no one to talk to and no one she could really trust.

Time went on and now two more months had passed. Reba's eyes were still slightly red from the beating she had taken from Braxton. Then one evening, she felt a funny feeling in her stomach, it felt like a butterfly. *What is that?* She thought to herself. *OMG, it's my baby.* At that point, she noticed that her mother was watching her every move and she began asking Reba many questions. She did everything she could to go around the questions that her mother would ask. "Reba did your cycle come on"? YES MA! "Reba you are looking funny are you felling ok"? YES MA!

Finally, one Sunday, on their way to church, Reba broke down and told her mother that she was having a baby. Regina was in such shock; she didn't say a word the rest of the way home from church. She just went in her room and cried. Reba felt so ashamed, even more, she was hurt because she knew that she had broken her mother's heart, but only if she really knew the whole story. As time went on, Reba's mother made sure that she didn't miss any of her doctor's appointments and they all were so excited to know that the baby was doing just fine.

Reba felt so relieved that her family finally knew and it seemed like the baby grew over night.

Time passed and it was now time for her baby to be born.

Reba pushed and she pushed, "The pain," Reba would cry out to her mother.

Her mother was right by her side, saying, "Baby, I know."

A few hours later, Reba's son was finally here. She looked into his eyes and called him, "Troy. Mom his name is Troy." Reba said, "God I thank you for my healthy baby boy."

Reba looked at her mother once again and said, "Mother, look at my son. Look, he is my life!" She knew that her life would be different, but all she could think of was that her little baby boy was here. She stared at her son. In her heart, he was the most handsome baby she ever laid eyes on. Troy was so soft, his hair jet black, and his skin smelled so pure and sweet. Reba whispered in her son's ear and said; "Hi Troy, it's me, your Mommy. It's no longer about me, it's about us now, and I'm going to love you for the rest of my life."

Getting up in the wee hours of the morning, warming bottles, and changing diapers, wasn't easy as it looked. At this point, Reba really realized that her life had changed forever. Thank God for her mother, she has really been there for her helping and teaching Reba how to be a mother. It was overwhelming for her at times, seeing her daughter and first grandchild; nonetheless, at the end of the day, Regina was a proud grandmother and mother.

After being home for some time with her newborn son, the time has come for Reba to return to school. Walking the halls, it felt as if all eyes were on her, all knowing that she had a baby. She could even hear the whispers, "Look who's back," were the words Reba could hear. That didn't bother her though; it was facing Braxton that scared her.

Two days passed and no Braxton, she felt relieved that she didn't see him in the halls. Day three, "Here we go," Reba said to herself. "I know this boy did not have his arms around Sharon and have the nerve to pass me like I don't even exist. He has lost his mind and this chick has the nerve to look at me and smile like, 'That's right, I got your man!'"

Although Reba got angry, a few minutes later, she had a flashback of all she had gone through with Braxton, and for the first time in a very long time, in her own way, she felt free. Sharon just didn't know how badly Reba wanted to tell her, *Girl you had better look at him real good because you have Satan's son on your arm, the child from hell!* "Thank you Lord at least I am at peace," Reba said to herself, and for some reason, she didn't feel afraid any more. "I am free," Reba said, "I am free, no more beatings, no looking in the room, I can now talk to anyone, and I don't have to look behind my back. I AM FREE."

One thing she did notice AND THAT was that not many guys in school were talking to her so much anymore. The first thing they would say was, "Didn't you have a baby by Braxton!"

Reba starting to feel like she was back where she started from and that was feeling like nobody again. You would think that having a baby was the worst thing that ever happened to anyone. Even Reba's friends no longer wanted to hang around her like they used to. At times, even they had smart things to say, "Girl, you can't go out this weekend, you got a baby at home." Reba started to learn very quickly who her friends really were and that was no one! High school had come to an end, and Reba graduated as a proud mother.

After finishing school, Reba went on with her life. While still living at home and thinking that no one cared on the outside began to take its toll on her, in her home, she had the love from her family, and that's all that mattered to her. Reba's attitude was, *I have a son, and I am not thinking about anything or anyone else.* She had a plan to move forward, and she did just that.

Reba began to work, making good money and eventually began meeting new friends. There was one friend in particular, Florence who she met when she at the clinic when she was pregnant. The two of them became very close, their children were born in the same month, just a week apart, and they were hoping that their children would be born on the same day. Reba just loved this girl; she was more than just a friend, she was like a sister. After they had their babies though, unfortunately, Reba and Florence didn't see each other for months. One day they ran into each other again, back at the clinic for their follow-up appointments, Florence had a little girl and Reba had her son. The two of them went through some things at the same time in their lives. Reba continued to work taking care of her son and started to move forward in her life.

Braxton never came around in the beginning of their son's life. His mother would call and come by to see her grandson. Reba and her mother were okay with that, until the day came that she asks if Troy could stay the night with her.

Reba instantly became defensive of her son; she felt like no one would hurt her baby, as she had been hurt. Reba knew that Braxton would be there and she didn't trust him at all, especially with her son. Deep down, she also knew that his mother wouldn't let anyone hurt her grandson. Nonetheless, Reba felt inside that it was just the principle behind it. *Why couldn't Braxton ask to see his son? Why did he have to use his mother?* Reba knew very well that he was behind this spend the night ordeal.

One thing about Reba though, she had a heart of gold, even though all the pain and abuse. Therefore, she finally allowed her baby to stay the night, but she made it very clear that she would be there bright and early in the morning to pick him up.

Reba didn't sleep well; she had her son on her

mind all night: *are they feeding him… did they change him… did they give him a bath…*just like a mother. Bright and early, her dad asked her, "Are you ready to go get my grandson?"

"Yes," she replied, and off they went.

Troy was home safe and sound and he was as bubbly and full of joy as always.

Now great things began to happen; Reba bought her first vehicle, a Honda Accord. Now 19 years old, still living at home, as we know, any time you still live under your parent's roof, no matter what age you are, you must abide by their rules and regulations.

At work, everybody was talking about the big party that was about to kick off at the Masonic Temple. Reba got up early that Saturday morning and cleaned the house; I mean cleaned it down! She had found out earlier in her life that a way to her mother's heart was to get her house cleaned, and the rest of the day was yours. Reba had a plan; *I'm going to hit the club tonight for the very first time.* Later that evening, Reba went to mother and said, "Mom, I want to get out tonight."

Her mother looked at her and said, "Reba, sure girl and have a good time!"

*Wow, she said yes.* Reba was so excited, she went in the bathroom, took a nice hot bath, and put lotion all over her body. *I'm going be a fine sister tonight*, Reba thought, as she curled her long hair. She finished her curls and then pinned the back of her long hair, leaving some curls hanging all down in the front of her face. She put her earrings on, followed by her Sassoon jeans, and her blue Members Only jacket. She took a little lip-gloss and put it on her lips, sprayed a little perfume, and she was ready to party. Reba was so excited, she went into her mother's room and said, "Mom, Troy had his bath, he has eaten and is now asleep and I'm getting ready to go out to the club. I won't be in too late."

Her mother looked at her and said, "Oh no, baby, take your time. I'm glad to know you won't be in too late and the baby has eaten and had a nice hot bath. Now, all you have to do is put his clothes on and take him with you to the club."

Reba's mouth dropped, her eyes were bigger than a ball, and all she could say was, "I'm sorry, Mommy, could you say that again!"

She said, "Yes, you heard me right; take your baby with you. Remember, you didn't ask if we would watch the baby for you. All I can say is be careful what you ask for."

Now y'all know, Reba's mother was wrong for that! Well, another life lesson learned for Reba. She turned around, and walked out of her mother's room, as mad as you know what. She started taking off the shoes, the Sassoon blue jeans, the earrings, and the lip-gloss. All she could do was sit on the edge of the bed and look at her son while he was sleeping and she said, "Well, baby, it really is all about you!"

Reba laid back, relaxed and watched TV, and here she comes, the one and only Ann, "You should've known better, that's what you get for not asking Mommy if somebody can watch Troy. See, you think you're grown, but you are not grown yet. You still live under Mommy's roof!"

"Lord, help me not to kill my sister," I know I pray this prayer quite often, "thank you for keeping my mind, my mouth shut and my fist open. AMEN!"

Well, it's Monday, back to work, and she had to face all of her friends that she'd told she'd be there. Reba knew that she couldn't avoid anyone because they all worked on the same line together. She was thinking all kinds of things, *because my mother or my sisters didn't want to babysit for me.* Reba had all kinds of thoughts running through her mind! *Thank you Lord,* she took a deep breath, not one person ever asked her why she wasn't there.

Everybody was too busy talking about the Masons, and how they partied, danced, drank, and had such a ball. Reba couldn't help but to think whom she could have met, or what she would have done that night. She was single now and she was looking! Her self-thoughts were, *I am young and fine; I will not go without having a man on my arms.*

Indeed, Reba was to the point in her life where she would do whatever it took to get what she wanted. She was now feeling that she was no longer the little girl that she used to be, and she kept that thought in her mind. *I am now grown and I will do as I please!*

# Chapter 4

# How low will you go

Although men were always asking her out on dates, Reba had her mind made up on what she was looking for. She was also still being very careful, not wanting that pain that she had experienced once before. One evening, she finally made it to Mansion Club, which everyone was talking about. She had on her high heels, a white mini skirt, and a nice purple halter-top. Hair down, her shoulder bouncing as she walked, Reba and her girls had it going on.

Although all the girls were on line waiting to get in, Reba had them all go in before her, since this was her first time ever in a club, and it was packed. She got very nervous, as it was her turn to walk through the door, but she kept herself together. The place was packed; the small dance floor was full of people. The bar was packed with men and women all over. Having checked out her surroundings, Reba was beginning to feel a little more comfortable. The men there were on her like never before, asking "Are you visiting the valley," or "I never seen you before, are you from around here?"

Reba's mother had kept her so secluded; she knew why many of them didn't know who she was. Nonetheless, in her own little way, she was enjoying the attention.

One man in particular caught her eye; he asked her to dance, and a few seconds later, they were on the dance floor. She danced with him, and oh, what a ball she had. After they danced, they exchanged phone numbers. Her girls were telling her who he was; "Reba, that's Richard, his family is one of the most well-known families in the valley. Girl, I heard they got money!"

Money was not on her mind; all Reba wanted was to be loved by someone who would accept her and her son Troy. Richard and Reba became close and the dating became serious after a year. She became pregnant, but this time, she wasn't afraid to tell her mother. Pregnant again and still not married, but Richard did ask her to marry him. Reba was so excited and couldn't wait to tell her mother and dad.

Regina was happy for her daughter but did have some concerns. "Reba sit, let's talk, you know, I want nothing more than the best for you, but you don't need to rush and marry because you are having another baby. Marriage is sacred before God. Honey, make sure you are in love and marrying for the right reasons."

Reba sat and looked at her mother and said, "Mom, I understand, but this is something I have always dreamed of and that's a family."

"Okay," her mother replied.

Reba thought about what her mother had said, she wondered if she was really *in love,* or did she *just love him.* However, it didn't matter to her. Even though she kept that thought in the back of her mind, Reba's main focus was having her second child, becoming another mother, and making sure that her children would be fine.

Preparing for her small wedding and working each day, Reba had a friend at work; he always kept her smiling, even on the days she didn't feel like it. Ken was one of a kind, Reba had always had her eyes on him, but she knew that he was married and they kept it as just friends. One day, Ken came to her and pulled her to the side, "What's up Ken?"

"Reba, look, you know that we are friends and have been for quite some time. Let me be honest with you and please take heed to what I'm about to say, please don't marry Richard. He is not the one for you."

Reba's heart dropped, "Why would you say that, Ken?"

"Listen, I'm in the streets, I know what goes on, and I just don't want to see you hurt."

Reba was devastated but it was too late, the wedding had been paid for and, she was pregnant and didn't want to have another child without the baby's father. All that day though, she thought about what Ken had said to her, and then the thought of her mother kept coming back, "Lord, what did I get myself into? Heavenly Father please keep me, my son, and my unborn child safe."

It was time for the wedding, Reba, now seven months pregnant, looking beautiful in her ivory gown with baby wreaths on the side of her hair, which she had pinned up. She had two beautiful bridesmaids, wearing matching cream-colored dresses.

However, when it came to the men, Reba was so upset, because she had asked Richard to make sure that his two groomsmen had matching suites on, of course, that didn't happen. Reba's first thought was, *that was a sure sign she should have listened to Ken and her mother.* Then, to top it all off, it stormed the day of the wedding. Reba had always heard the old people say that if it rains on your wedding day, your marriage will not work... all Reba could think was, *what a day!*

After the wedding, many people came to the reception; she even saw Ken and his wife. He looked at her, came over, and whispered in her ear; "I wish you well, if you ever need me, I will be there."

She smiled and said, "Thank you that means a lot." Reba was looking around for her new husband but couldn't find him anywhere, until she looked over and noticed Richard and some guys going in and out the door quite often. She never said a word to him, even though she kept a close eye on them.

Reba and Richard never had a honeymoon; they stayed in a hotel for the night and what a night it was. He was so intoxicated, and the Lord only knows whatever else he was doing, he laid across the bed and fell asleep in his clothing. Reba just shook her head and slept in the other bed, thinking to herself, *Thank you Lord, we have double beds.*

There were many nights when Reba cried, wanting to go home to her family. It was not easy on her and her son Troy living in the basement of her in-laws home. There were days when Richard didn't even come home. Reba and Troy slept in the bedroom together downstairs. When Richard would finally come in, Reba would let him have it! "Why did you marry me? Where have you been? Why do you smell funny?"

The smell didn't smell like another woman, it had a foul order. "What's wrong with your eyes, Richard? What's wrong with you? What happened to you, to us?"

Reba never got an answer from him; he would do well for a couple of days, and then disappear again for days at a time. Reba was trying to hold on and make a plan, but she was heartbroken once again, and this time there were three of them.

It was time, and the baby was on the way. When Reba went into labor, Richard was there by her side. After fifteen hours, their son was born. His name was Isaiah and just as handsome as he could be. Troy was now a big brother, and Reba was a very proud mother, in spite all she has been going through.

Reba and Isaiah made it home, Troy was with her mother in Goshen, and Reba couldn't wait to see her baby and mom. Richard stayed home with her and the baby; he was a lot of help. She felt great watching him with his firstborn, it was beautiful, and for once, she was thinking that she finally had a family and maybe this marriage would work.

Reba's family all came by to bring Troy home and to see the new little man in her life. Nonetheless, you could feel the tension in the house with her mother and in-laws. Regina didn't stay long and it saddened Reba's heart to see her mother and sisters leaving. She wanted so much to tell them all what she had been through and she truly wanted to pack all of their things and leave with them.

Although Reba remained silent, she held them all

so tight; they knew something wasn't right. Ann asked, "Reba, are you alright?"

Dropping her head, she said, "Yes, sis, I'll be fine."

"Reba, you know you can come home," Ann said.

"Yes, sis, I know, thank you." Reba replied.

Tears were falling down her face as she watched them drive off. Not seeing Richard for days again, Troy would help his mommy as much as he could for a four year old. He knew how to pass the Pampers and pass the bottle and he knew when his baby brother needed that binky.

Months had now passed by and Reba was back at work, Troy in pre-K, and Isaiah in daycare. Nothing changed with Richard, he would go to work, in and out, and he would come and go.

One day at work, Ken came to Reba and said, "Reba, how are you doing?"

"I don't know, what's going on, Ken." Reba looked at him, fighting back her tears. "Ken, please tell me what's going on because I have no clue, is there another women in his life?"

"No, Reba."

"What Ken, please, you have to tell me, I can't take it anymore."

"Let's talk after work."

Reba agreed because she knew she was about to lose it, and she was afraid to hear what was happening with her husband. Hours had gone by and she waited patiently for Ken to come through the gate. Her heart began to pump fast as he got closer to her. "Reba, follow me, let's go somewhere away from the job."

*My Life Story*

Reba trusted Ken, so she followed him off the premises and went to a plaza down the street.

Since it was a warm afternoon, they got out of their cars and sat on the bench. "Are you okay, Reba?" Ken asked.

"No, Ken, please just tell me what's going on!"

"Reba, Richard is on crack."

"CRACK! What is that?"

"It's a drug that just came out, they say that after one hit, you must have more."

Reba cried, "Why, I just don't get it, why? What am I to do Ken, can I help him?"

"Reba, he has to want to help himself."

Reba and Ken went their separate ways. Ken really cared about Reba, they had been friends for a long time, and he didn't want to see her hurt any longer. He felt bad that he had to be the one to tell her the truth.

Heartbroken, she had to get her face together before she picked up her children; she never wanted Troy to see his mommy cry. When they entered the door, there stood Richard, his mother and sister. Just by the look they gave her, Reba felt like she was the subject of the conversation before she came in the house. She smiled, took her children, and went downstairs, like always.

It was to the point that Reba really hated being there. She could hear everything that was said about her. Her mother-in-law's room was above her bedroom, one day Reba heard her mother-in-law and sister-in-law saying, "I don't know why he married her in the first place, she already had a child, we just need to tell them to move."

Although Reba wanted to go up those stairs and go

off on both of them, she kept herself together. She had always been taught that there was a time and place for everything. Reba began to save every penny and dime she had, preparing to move into her own place.

Then one day, Isaiah became very sick with a fever and he didn't want to eat much, so she took him to the doctor, and he was prescribed some medication. He had to be indoors for a few days. Reba couldn't take time off from the job. Even though Richard was home, she didn't want to ask him, but she had no other choice, "Richard, are you going to be home today?"

"Yes, what's up?"

"It's Isaiah; he is sick and doesn't need to be out. Can I leave him home with you?"

"Yes, why would you ask me that? He is my son."

Reba gave Richard the craziest look. "Okay Richard, please take care of my son. If he gets worse, call me at work, please."

Reba and Troy left, she dropped him off to school, and off to work she went. Hours had gone by and she became worried. She just felt like something was wrong.

When Ken came in on his shift, he said, "Reba, you look like you don't feel good, are you okay?"

She looked at him and replied, "I don't know, but something just doesn't feel right. Ken, I need you to be honest with me, do you know where Richard hangs out when he's not home?"

"Not really, Reba, but I hear a lot of people hang out on Twin Avenue, in those apartments, but I'm not sure if that's where he hangs out.

*My Life Story*

Reba replied, "I know what his car looks like!"

She began to call Richard at the house, no answer, she tried quite a few more times, and finally his mother answered.

"Hi, is Richard there?"

"No, he and Isaiah aren't here. They left this morning."

Reba became very angry, "I am sorry, did you say this morning? He knows that Isaiah was not supposed to leave the house, he is sick!"

"Well, why would leave the baby with him?" Richard's mother asked.

Reba became even angrier and said, "WHY WOULDN'T I ASK HIM, HE'S THE FATHER OF OUR CHILD?"

Reba knew something was wrong. Her motherly instinct had been working her all day; she really didn't know how powerfully this drug takes over a person's mind. She left work early and went straight to Twin Avenue. She knew of the apartments but had no clue about them. She found them though, and there it was, Richard's car.

Since Reba didn't know which apartment or door to go to, she began to knock on every one of the doors. She was not going to stop until she found her son. Finally, she found the right door; she could smell that same smell that Richard would come home with on his clothing. Banging on the door as hard as she could, she could hear people talking, and someone finally opened the door.

"IS RICHARD IN THERE?"

The man said, "No, he's not here."

All Reba could say was, "I know he is in there and if he doesn't bring my son out of there, I will be calling the police, and I mean what I say."

Reba was so angry, by the time she got back to her car, here comes Richard with Isaiah, his eyes big and just smelling. "Richard, I know you didn't bring my son out here to this apartment, where you do your drugs! Are you crazy?"

Reba wanted to just slap the mess out of him, but all she could think about was her son. As she was putting him in her car, Richard was saying, "Reba, I am sorry."

Her reply was, "Yes, I do know that Richard, you are sorry as Hell. Where did you have my baby in this stink apartment?"

"I had him in that back room with the dogs. He was fine."

Reba lost it and tried her best to knock the crap out of him with her fist; she was ready to fight. However, she stopped when she heard her baby cry. By the time she looked back, Richard was gone.

Reba picked up Troy from school and off to the house they went. When she went to get Isaiah out of the car seat, he was drenched and had not been changed all day. After she got into the house, she changed her baby gave both of them a nice hot bath, got them settled in, Reba went upstairs, and began to tell her mother-in-law what took place. Tears were rolling down her face and you could see that Reba was hurt and burned out; pouring out her heart to her mother-in-law, telling her that Richard needs help. However, Reba was very shocked at the reply she received.

"Reba, he is a grown man, he has the right to do

what he wants to do. What do you want me to do?"

Reba looked at her in disbelief, thinking this family is just not right. "Thank you," Reba replied, and left her room. Downstairs, she went grabbing for both of her babies. Once again, she felt trapped and that she had lost her soul; her heart was broken. She became very depressed and decided that she had enough and was leaving for good.

Reba called her mother crying, "Mommy, please can me and my babies come home? I can't take it anymore."

Regina replied, "Baby, I was just waiting for you to call. Yes, come home, and bring my babies."

Reba began packing everything she could fit in her white Honda. The trunk was completely stuffed and one side of the back seat was packed as well. She was able to put her baby Isaiah on the other side, while Troy rode in the front in his car seat, smiling at his mother.

Then Reba shouts out, "Babies, lets so home," and off they went.

As she looked through her rear view mirror, she felt like so much weight had just lifted off her shoulders. When she left that house, not one person was there, and Reba didn't care one bit, why should she? Not one person in that house cared about her or her children and that's exactly how she was feeling as she looked at that house driving away.

Because she knew that Troy was too young to be in the front, she took her time traveling the back roads. Once again, Reba was doing what she had to do to survive with her children. Goshen, New York, Reba looked at her two little men and said, "We made it, and we are home."

As she pulled into the driveway, her mom, dad,

and sisters all greeted them at the door. Reba sat with her mother and told her all that had taken place, even how he had her son in the crack house.

Regina became very angry and she yelled now, "HOW LOW WILL YOU GO? Reba, you have been through so much in your life in such a short time, I am grateful and have been keeping you lifted up before the Lord asking him to shield you and protect you and I'm grateful that he has done just that, in bringing you home. Baby, it's now time to heal, and get your life in order. Reba, you know the Word, you grew up in the church, trust God, and he will make a way."

"Yes, Mommy, I know that he will, I have been praying," she replied.

Reba took a week off from work and relaxed, enjoying family, trying to adjust and regroup with her new life to come. She got news that Richard had been looking for her and the kids. All of her girls knew not to say one word to him and they didn't, because they knew that she had enough of what he had put her through.

With just a few more days before she had to return to work, Reba ask her mother to ride with her to get the rest of her things from Richard's house, praying that he would not be there.

Ann said, "Sis, I am riding with you and Mom."

Reba felt even more relieved, knowing that she didn't have to face them alone. As her mother pulled up to the house, Reba took a deep breath and got out of the car. As she walked to the front door, she was saying, "Lord, please just let me get my things and be able to leave."

Richard's sister answered the door.

Reba said softly, "Shelly, I just wanted to come and get the rest of my things."

His sister gave her the most evil look and said, "Wait a minute," and closed the door in her face.

Looking back at her mother's car, Reba could hear her mother and sister saying, "They better not be starting any mess with her, if so, it's going down!"

Now Reba was really starting to get upset, because she was not one to like confrontations and she knew that her sister Ann was not one to play with. The door reopened and it was Richard, "What do you want?"

"I would like to just get the rest of the kids' and my clothing, that's all I would like to do," she replied.

"You're not getting a damn thing out this house," he said loudly.

That was it; Reba lost her temper and began to yell back. "I did all I could do to hold this marriage down, I will not bring my boys up with drugs around them."

The next thing you see is his mother and sister coming out of the house. Reba could see her mother getting out of the car yelling, "I know good and well, you don't think you're going to put your hand on my daughter," she yelled at his mother.

Ann jumps out of the car and declared to Richard's sister, "If you think you're going to jump my sister, me and you are getting ready to rumble. Nobody is putting their hand on my sister and I mean that."

Richard got even closer to Reba and before you knew it, he was on the ground, and she was letting him have it with all her might.

His mother yelled, "GET OUT OF MY YARD, ALL OF YOU BEFORE I CALL THE POLICE!"

Ann was yelling, "Get him, sis, don't let him up!"

Reba was so mad, because he told her that he threw the rest of their things in the trash and he sold the TV she bought. Tears rolling down her eyes, "Richard, you will reap what you sow. How can you throw those babies' clothes away? You have no heart."

They got back in Regina's car and left. Her mother and sister gave her comfort all the way back to Goshen. "Reba, it's okay. At least you and my grandbabies are safe and in a good place, you're home."

Ann added, "Hey girl, look on the bright side, girl you punched him a couple of good times and when he tripped and fell on the ground, you sucker punched him in his eye and lip. In the morning, both will be swollen, hard as you were hitting."

Reba giggled, wiping her eyes, "Thanks sis, coming from you, I must not have done too badly."

The time had come, and Reba knew that she had to return to work. Months went by and she focused on her life, every now and then, she would hang out and enjoy herself. Then one night she saw Richard, he was looking so bad, it broke her heart to see him looking the way he did.

He yelled her name, "Reba, can I talk to you for a minute?"

Her girls looked at her and asked, "Do you want us to handle this, girl? You know we are not afraid to fight a man!"

In her soft voice, Reba said, "No, let me see what he wants, but stay close."

"Okay," one of her friends replied.

"What's up, Richard, what do you want?"

"Reba, I want you. I need my family back."

She replied, "That is gone, Richard, let's face it, you were never there for me or my children. I'll never say it was a mistake because I have a beautiful son out of the mess you put me through. Thank you for my son, but I will be filing for a divorce and I pray that you get your life in order."

Reba could see the tears running down his face but one thing she had to learn the hard way and that was to never go backward, because she knew that the pain would never end. Reba and her girls got in the car and that's when she broke down crying, "All I ever wanted in my life was someone to love me, why can't I have a real man? That's not asking too much is it?"

"No, it's not," her friends replied. Then they all gave her a group hug and held her in their arms.

"Reba, it's not asking a lot, but for some reason we always seem to pick the wrong one," her friend Flo stated.

Weeks went by and Reba kept in her mind what Flo had said to her that night. She thought about it over and over again, and then became angry, "It's time to change things around in my life," Reba shared with her friend Flo, "Girl, you know what, I am so tired of these men thinking they can do what they want and get away with it, if they run a game so can I."

The look Flo gave her, at first, she was lost for words, but finally she managed to respond, "Girl, have you lost your mind?"

Reba said, "Flo, just sit back and watch, and you will see, I going to show these men that we can run a game just as well as they can."

# Chapter 5

# Money won't buy love

Reba had one thing on her mind and that was trying to find love. However, at the same time, she kept one thing in front of her mind and that was that she would not let another man get away with hurting her feelings. Months had passed by since her episode with Richard and she was focused on herself and her boys.

Then great news came and that was that her sister Ann was getting married. Ann getting her wedding plans together was a great feeling for Reba, seeing her sister marrying someone that she loved. She was proud of Ann, but even more so, she was happy that her sister didn't have to go through the pain that she went through.

Reba wondered how Ann did that, no pain, not in and out of relationships. One thing Reba knew was that Ann always stayed in the church and she was faithful to the Lord. *Why didn't I stay in church like her*, Reba thought to herself, *why did I fall by the waste side? Was it because of the people I was with, always saying girl that party was off the chain and I just wanted to fit in?* Reba couldn't figure it out but she had gotten to the point where she wasn't giving up on love either, *if Ann found love, then so can I.*

The wedding day came. Ann looked so beautiful and all of her girls were beautiful as well. Dad was looking as in shape as he could be, with Mama Regina holding his arm, looking gorgeous as ever. Reba had a date, a handsome man, tall 6'3", and nice shapely body. His name was Charles. He worked for UPS and had been on the job for 15 years; he was the only child and seemed to be very charming.

Although Reba had known Charles for a while through other people, she didn't pay him much attention until two weeks prior to the wedding. One afternoon, she had decided to grab a bite to eat before heading back to Goshen after work. Stopping at a fast food restaurant, she noticed him at the counter.

Charles turned and said, "Hello, Reba, how are you? It's been a long time."

"I am well," she replied softly.

The two of them stayed in the restaurant talking and laughing for quite some time. He paid for her meal and they exchanged numbers. After that, they began talking on the phone for hours at a time. Reba became very impressed with him and they went on a few dates, with no pressure.

Ann's wedding was beautiful and elegant; Charles was looking good, dressed in his double-breasted suit with sharp looking shoes that matched his suit. That man was fly and clean cut and Reba couldn't keep her eyes off of him.

Her plan was kicking into effect, *victim one, let's see how long this could go,* she thought. *I am going to get whatever I can, just like it was done to me.*

Not wanting to settle down, Reba began meeting quite a few men in her days, just enjoying the single life for once, but she was keeping Charles close by. She dated a well-known doctor, an attorney, a pro football player, and a business owner. Fancy cars, luxury hotels, five-star restaurants, Reba was starting to learn that all of the money in the world doesn't bring happiness or love, but it does bring a controlling atmosphere and that was not what she was looking for in her life.

Yes, Reba wanted for nothing in those relationships; her boys lacked for nothing. One even moved her and her children into their own place, and Reba didn't have to work. However, soon after they moved, he became very possessive and out of control. "Where have you been?" He demanded, "I called you and you didn't answer. I put money in your account, what did you buy?"

Reba was a different woman at this time in her life and she came back at him, "Wait a minute, I didn't ask you for anything, all that you have done was by your choice. We are not married and I owe you nothing! And another thing, I will not let another man control me so the best thing we can do at this point is go our separate ways."

The look that Reba gave him, he knew that the best thing to do was to leave it alone or his job could be on the line. Although Reba remained friends with Charles through all of this, she was really enjoying the single life. She had it going on, not finding love, but just enjoying being spoiled by men.

One of her men had a nice boat, it could sleep four comfortably, and he would keep them on the Hudson River, keeping money in her account, paying her bills, including her car payments. He was falling in love with her and she knew it; she cared about him a lot. He was an older man, very caring, and loving, more of a sugar daddy to Reba, but she adored him and didn't want to hurt him. She frequently told him gently, "Please don't fall in love; I am not ready to settle down. I've been there and done that, love hurts, at least in my world."

Each time Reba found that someone wanted to get close to her heart, she would walk away. She knew that some of the men she dated would give her and her boys the world but she wasn't looking for the world, she was looking for something special and different in her man. Deep down, she knew that all the men she was dating were either trying to buy her love or they were running the game, just as she was.

Reba remembered the words of God: **Proverbs 18:22 "*He who* finds a wife finds a good *thing,* and obtains favor from the Lord."**

Reba knew in her heart that she was a good thing, out of all these men that she dated, not one ever mentioned the name Lord, and if she brought up church or the Lord, they would always change the subject, and then it was time for her to go. Reba didn't care about the money; she had that working hard every day. She was able to take care of her boys on her own. Reba had love and she wanted to share it with the right man. Even as a young girl, it had always been her dream to one day have a family with a good husband.

She watched her mother and the love that she shared in their house. It was because of her that Reba knew how to love. She never heard her mother complain, not one day, they didn't even know when she wasn't feeling well. Dinner was always on the stove when Dad and all of us got home. Regina is a strong woman, a woman of God, a praying mother, and her children knew that. In many ways, Reba has followed in her mother's footsteps in the caring and loving world. While Reba also knew the word of God, she was determined to find her love on her own. She and her children were now living in New Windsor, New York, and she decided to leave the company that she had been working for and start a new life.

Now free, Reba had her eyes back on Ken, *My goodness he is a fine piece of dark chocolate.* Reba's heart would melt when she saw him and OMG, don't let him smile his pearly white teeth and thick lips, and let's not forget to mention the perfectly chiseled body that would make you go crazy. The funny thing is, Ken had his eyes on Reba as well, and she knew he was watching her.

Reba would go to the Mansion Club every now and again, and Ken would be there; he would watch her every move. There were times when he would come over to her and whisper in her ear, "Looking good girl, don't hurt them tonight."

"Oh yeah, he will be my first victim on my new brick house diva journey," Reba said to herself! *Mr. Dark chocolate needs to watch out because Ms. Reba is truly on the prowl.* Ken and Reba danced a couple of times that night. Her girl Flo would just smile; she knew that Reba had always had a crush on Ken, but she would never say a word.

Ken was another one who was doing very well for himself; he worked two good jobs and he had it going on! Reba and Ken exchanged numbers that night; she even found out that Ken and his wife had separated.

Reba felt like Ken would be a great catch; he was right up her alley. They went on quite a few dates, but one night as he was talking with her on the phone, he told her, "Reba if you hadn't married Richard, I would have ask you to marry me. I am in love with you."

Reba's mouth dropped; she didn't know what to say at first. "Ken, what's wrong? Why can't we try to start a relationship now?"

He replied, "I can't, Reba I am close to that family and it wouldn't feel or be right at all."

Reba didn't care; she still wanted Ken. Whatever it took, she was going to try, hoping that he would change his mind.

Since Ken and Reba were both still married at the time, they would sneak off and meet in other towns to be together. They even became intimate and this went on for a couple of years. Reba knew that Ken was a player; she was the one who forgot that she was playing the game as well and that's because she was really feeling for him. As time went on though, Ken would begin to cancel the plans they had made. Reba knew what time it was, but whenever he wanted to be with her, she would still be there.

One day, Reba thought about what she was doing and said, "No more. I am not a hooker and I don't stand on nobody's corner."

Then one day, Ken called Reba out the blue and said, "Hey babe, what's up with you? Are you busy?"

Reba replied, "No."

"Come meet me at our usual place."

"Sure," she replied, "at the Marriott in Mount Vernon, New Jersey?"

"Yes," he said, "how about 3:00 pm?"

"That's great," Reba hung up her phone and realized, *After all these years, nothing has changed, but the year and the date, except this time, he will be in for a rude awaking, because I will not be there!*

Hours passed and Ken finally called her back, "Baby, where are you at?" he asked.

"I am at home where I should be."

"Reba, I thought we agreed to meet."

"Yes, we did," she replied. "Ken, listen, you know how I feel about you and you know what I want, you have made your point. It has been two years and nothing has changed. I don't want to be your door mat any longer, besides I hear that you are talking to one of the twins."

"REBA, wait!"

"Ken, no it's over and done with. Thank you for the beautiful times we shared but it's time to move on." Reba hung up her phone, never hearing from Ken again. Eight months later, she learned that he and the young lady had moved in together and that he had filed for his divorce.

Reba was saddened by this news, she felt horrible that she allowed herself to do the things that she did to try to keep him. Ken told Reba in the beginning that he loved her but wouldn't be able to been seen with her because of the relationship he had with her EX family. Reba was glad that she no longer lived in the same town and didn't have to face him anymore. She began working at a well know car dealership selling Toyotas. Reba became the first top female seller and she began a program called CAC. This program helped people with bad credit obtain new cars. She did so well, she had her own television commercial on major stations and she had news ads. Reba was happy with her life, spending time with her children, and moving forward, things were finally looking good for her and her boys.

The crew she worked with was great, loving, and they were a team. Regina was glad to see her daughter happy, for once, doing well for herself, not stressed or depressed. Reba would spend even more time with her mom, dad, and younger siblings, something that she didn't do much of in her past.

During that time, Reba's dad became very ill and soon afterwards, he passed. She once again became depressed. Her dad was not only her hero, but he was her protector. In her eyes, her dad, William, was amazing; even though he was her stepfather, she loved him as if he were her real dad. He always kept a smile on her face, and he would always have those cards, checkers, or even a Monopoly board ready when he knew she was coming over and Reba had always loved it. There was nothing like spending time with him and mom in the kitchen, at the table playing one of those games.

Reba believed that the love both of her parents showed her was food to her soul; besides, there was nothing like Mom's good home cooked meals. Reba missed her dad and she knew that a part of life wouldn't be the same. She felt that way because he was the only man who had always been true to her and the only man she could trust. Reba will always remember the words he gave her a long time ago when others would pick on her in school. He said, "Reba, no matter what, always hold your head up. Stop looking down, you can't find your way looking down. Holding your head up means strength and I know you have that, so show the world that you are strong, no matter what, keep your head up."

There were many times with all she had been through that she walked with her head down and people took advantage of her. But now, Reba walks with her head up and she says, "I am the head and not the tail! I will not be another door mat," or so she thought.

# Chapter 6

## Here we go again

Reba had done some traveling for her job, and finally making it home after a week of training, she ran into Charles once again, this time it was at a gas station. "Charles, how are you?"

"Hi, I am well."

"That's great, you are looking good."

"Thanks. So, Reba, tell me, did you remarry?"

"No, I am single, working hard, trying to stay focused."

"What about you?"

"No, I haven't found the right one yet."

"Oh, okay," she replied.

Charles was always a gentleman to Reba. While he was laid back and stayed to himself, and as you know, he and Reba had dated at one point, but she wasn't quite ready to settle down at that time.

Once again, Charles took a chance and asked her out. This time, she was ready, they were enjoying one another's company, and their relationship became serious enough for them to live together. Charles was great and the boys really enjoyed him. They were all happy. Reba became pregnant again. Troy was now eight years old, and Isaiah was four. Reba was praying for a little girl, Charles was neutral about the pregnancy, he wasn't sure if he was ready for a child. Reba told him, "Whether you are ready or not, I am having my child. I never gave up my two boys and I am not giving this one up either."

      Charles starting changing as the months went by, and he start coming home a little later than usual, "Here we go again," Reba said, "why does it always end up this way?"

      Seven months had gone by and things got worse in their relationship. Although they were truly in love with one another, as time went on, she found out that Charles was also a drug user. Indeed, it is hard at times to realize an addict, because some can hide it very well. Reba soon found out that he was a working addict, better known as, "FUNCTIONING ADDICTS."

      The relationship had reached the point where he was not bringing any money home each week and Reba found herself going to his job to try and catch him before he cashed his check, because then it was too late. He already owed half the people money back that he would borrow for the week. All she could do was wait in line. Charles would be left with $50.00 sometimes. This went on for some time, Reba would talk to him, "Charles, please try to get some help." However, that was like talking in one ear and out the other.

The time was finally here and Reba went into labor. Her mother didn't live too far away from her so the boys stayed with her while she had the baby. Charles was right there by her side. Reba got her wish, it was a girl, and her name was Stacy. Charles was so excited and a proud dad he was.

It was getting late and Charles had Reba's car, "Babe you know I have to work in the morning so I am going home, call the house if you need anything."

"Okay," she replied.

Reba held Stacy all night, until it was time for her to go to the nursery. Then Reba prayed, "Lord, please help me and my three children. I see where this is going again, Father I am tired, I know I have asked for your help plenty of times but I want out and I just want peace for my three children. Father I am scared and I can't do this without you, please don't you ever leave me like my daddy did. Now you're the only man I have that I can really trust, Amen."

On the third day, it was time for her to go home and she had not seen or heard from Charles. Her heart was broken once again. *How could he leave my baby and me in the hospital like this?*

Reba called her mother but she had not seen or heard from him either. Reba now has to call his mother, and that's a story in itself. Charles' mother didn't care for Reba at all. She felt like Reba was taking her child away from her, the love she had for her son was unreal at times. She always felt like it didn't matter what he did, as long as he was at home or in her house, and not hanging in the street getting into trouble. Reba called her and explained to her that she had not seen Charles since the baby was born and she needed a way home, "I have been discharged."

Janie, Charles mother, replied, "Well, I don't know where he is at and I don't get off until 5:00 pm. Once the doors close here, I have to finish up my paper work and you're just going to have to wait until I get there."

Reba looked at the clock and dropped her head. The nurse came in and she explained what was going on.

The nurse was so kind, "It's going to be okay sweetheart. I'll let the nurses on the next shift know that you will be leaving but are waiting for your ride."

Reba kept Stacy in the room with her, not wanting her baby to leave her site. Finally, her door opened and it was Charles mother, "You ready?"

"Yes," Reba replied.

His mother didn't help her lift or carry anything, the car was quiet, even Stacy didn't make a sound. She even had the nerve to light a cigarette in the car with the windows closed. She had no respect at all and the fact that Reba had just given birth to her first grandchild, who was resting in the back, made no difference to her, as she continued puffing that cigarette.

Reba was so glad when she pulled up to the door of her apartment, thinking, *Thank God, that smoke was killing my baby and me.* Well, Reba thought to herself, *She knows I have the baby in the car seat, plus I have bags, and I have to walk up all these stairs, maybe she will get out and help me.*

That she did, in her own way. She got out of her car, put the baby bags on the sidewalk, said, "Have a good night," and off she went.

Reba cried, struggling up the stairs, in pain, she could feel her stomach knotting up, but by the grace of GOD, they made it to the top of the stairs. Once she was settled in, she called her mom and told her what all had taken place

Regina was angry, "Reba, don't let me go there with that woman."

"No Mom, this one I have to deal with on my own."

Her mother simply said, "Okay, but you let me know."

"I will, Mom."

Her mother kept the kids the rest of the week, giving her some time to get herself together. Day five, she heard the front door open and Reba knew it wasn't the kids as she walked to the front door; it was Charles. She wanted to jump on him, she was just that angry, but she couldn't.

The two of them just stared at each other and then he finally opened his mouth, "Reba, I am truly sorry, baby, please forgive me."

She looked at him as if he was crazy, "Forgive you for what? Leaving me and our baby in the hospital the way you did."

He slipped over to the couch to have a seat, not knowing what she was going to do.

Reba lost it, "SORRY, yes you are, I am so sick and tired of hearing, 'Reba I am sorry, Reba I didn't mean to hurt you, Reba you know I love you...' ENOUGH," she yelled. "Love is not supposed to hurt but that's all men seem to know how to do! I tell you what, take your sorry ASS, and get the Hell out of my house right now. Call your trifling mama and tell her to come pick you up. While you are at it, make sure you tell her that I SAID IT BETTER BE BEFORE 6:00 PM OR YOU AND YOUR CLOTHING WILL BE SITTING ON THE CURB UNTIL SHE GETS HERE!"

Reba meant every word she said, Charles went into the room and began looking for her luggage. She went in the kitchen and brought him some trash bags, "I don't know why you think you are going to use my traveling bags, but that's the wrong answer, not today buddy. Where ever you were at for those five days, you should have asked them for a bag!"

Charles was looking like he had not slept in days, "Can I just talk to you; I need help. I have a drug problem."

Reba replied, "Find a meeting, find a rehab place, Charles, but for the first time in my life, I am not going through this anymore, I now have three kids. In the beginning, I tried to help you, but you didn't want my help. I found places for you to go get help and told you that I would stay by your side, even go to meetings with you and what did you do, you listened to your mama instead."

"My mama said I don't have a problem like most people do, at least I can keep a job."

"Well, I tell you what, you and your mama figure out what y'all are going to do from here."

He knew that she meant it.

"Charles, I have three children to raise, from this point on, I'll be damned if I am going to let any man disrespect my home or my children. We have been together for years and you know what; yea, it hurts but life goes on. Oh, and another thing, how much longer is it going to take you to get the rest of your things?"

Reba heard the horn blowing, she went to the window, and low and behold, it was his mother. "I see she came right away, did you know she left me and your daughter in the hospital over eight hours and I had no way home."

Charles looked shocked when she said that. "Reba, what did you just say?"

She replied, "YOUR MOTHER MADE ME AND YOUR BABYSIT IN THE HOSPITAL WHILE SHE TOOK HER SWEET TIME TO PICK US UP! That's what I said, close your mouth, Charles, the apple does not fall far from the tree."

Reba held her hand out as he grabbed his bags, she loudly cleared her throat as he looked at her, "What is it, Reba?"

"Aren't you forgetting something?"

Keeping his head down, Charles looked back at the closet and dresser drawers, "No, I am not."

"OH, YES YOU ARE," she replied, "my keys to my car and my house keys! Just to let you know, I will be changing my locks on my house door."

His mother was incessantly blowing the horn, as if she had lost her mind. Reba fought back her tears, as she locked her door, stood there, and then went to the window, peeking out, looking at Charles, saying to herself, "He was good to me and I tried but I am tired and once again, I am alone."

Charles never gave up; he would come by and spend time with all the kids. Reba was often wishing things would be different and hoping he had changed, or was at least working on it. One afternoon, she got off work and noticed that Charles was standing at her door; it startled her. "Charles, what are you doing here?"

He was looking very strange, he had a look that she had never seen on his face before, and she became a little nervous, "What's wrong?"

Charles didn't answer at first, she opened the doors, "Come in, have a seat."

"Reba, I need help. I really need some money."

"Charles, are you not working anymore?"

"No, I got fired."

"What happened?"

"Reba, I don't want to get into that, can you help me?"

Deep in her heart, she wanted to, but she knew that this would be taking away from her children and not only that, she did not want to support his habit either. "Charles, I am sorry, but I just don't have it. You really need to try and get some help." Reba talked to Charles for a while and then she realized that he didn't want to hear anything she was saying. He had an urge, he needed that fix, and he wanted out, not to hear her speech.

"Reba, look, I understand everything you are saying, but I have to go." Charles got up, kissed her on the forehead, and walked out the door, driving off in his mother's car.

Reba held Stacy in her arms, tightly kissing her, telling her that Mommy will never hurt you. When the boys came home after school, all she wanted to do was hold them and tell them how much Mommy loved them, and that's exactly what she did. She played games with them all night long; they even had her playing train. She would ride them on her back around the house, just as her mother had done with them. However, at night, she would cry from being so lonely and wanting a better life for her children.

# Chapter 7

# Living on the Edge

*Why Lord? Why do I keep choosing these men, I always seem to pick the wrong ones.* Now with three children, Reba thought about moving out of state, thinking that South Carolina might be the place for her to try to make her new home for her and the children. Reba had a $30,000.00 settlement that came through for her being in a car accident with her two babies. Normally she would put both of them in the back seat, but for some reason Troy was being very persistent.

"Mommy I'm a big boy now and my feet can reach the floor," he would say. So she decides to put him in the front, buckle him up and put Isaiah behind her so Troy could give him his bottle if he gets a little cranky. Well thank God she did. A drunk driver slammed in the back of her pushing the backside up to the front seat where Troy was sitting. It was the most horrible thing to see. All she could was hold on to her babies and thank GOD for sparing their lives. This caused a five-car pile-up!  After receiving her money, she sat with her mother and told her that for better or worse, she needed to make this move. She knew she needed a change in her life. Her mother, Regina, begged her not to leave; she felt in her heart that she wasn't ready to make such a big move.

Nonetheless, Reba was determined to try to make it on her own. Her mother asked if she would just leave some money in the bank, as a safety blanket, in case of hard times.

She replied, "Mom, I am a big girl now, I think I can manage my money well."

However, since Regina was born and raised in South Carolina and had family there, she felt that Reba would be safe and surrounded by loved ones there. With that being said, off they went with the car packed down. The car was so full they couldn't get any more in the truck or the back seat; the two little ones were in the back and Troy in the front.

They finally made it to South of the Border and the two little men were so excited, they had never seen anything like it before. "Mommy, Mommy," they yelled, "look at the big man, is he a cowboy?"

Reba laughed, "No my babies, he is not."

Finally, in Columbia, South Carolina, Reba was worn out, thirteen hours of driving alone with three babies was a long rough trip for her. She stayed with a family member until she got her own place, not needing to work right away, because she figured she would live off her settlement for a while.

Reba started realizing her money was going quickly since she was helping others, as well as spending it on her own bills. With the kids in school, she felt like it was time for her to get her own place and so she did.

She found a two-bedroom apartment, not too far from one of the technical colleges, where many of the students lived. Reba was okay with that because she stayed to herself. Soon after that, she met a new friend; his name was Leroy. He seemed to be kind and gentle and they would hang out from time to time when she had a babysitter. Leroy and Reba became more than friends, he moved in with her, helping with her bills.

Her family finally came to visit her from New York and Reba was so happy. One day, her mother pulled her in the kitchen and said girl, "Where did you find him at?"

Reba was shocked and didn't know what to say.

"Reba, I was praying that you would just take your time and find yourself," her mother was coming down on her hard, but Reba knew she was telling her the truth. "Child, I hope you had enough sense to put some of your money up."

Not saying one word, Regina looked at her daughter and walked away.

Reba was saddened by her mother's words, as we all know the truth does hurt, but like most, she stuck with it and kept her mother's words close to her heart.

Things were getting rough for her in Columbia. Leroy was doing crazy baby mama drama things, guess he thought he could have the best of both worlds. Reba soon found out that he too was on drugs, sniffing cocaine.

Once again, Reba packed her things and moved to the other side of town without him, leaving his things in the apartment. Still trying to make South Carolina her home, her money was running low and she knew she had to do something and quick. She also didn't want to call her mother and tell her that she had failed and should have listened to her by leaving money in a bank in New York.

Reba would go job hunting; taking Stacy with her, while she filled out applications. She would always make it back home before the boys got home from school. One day, she got a call from one of the hospitals asking her to come in for an interview; knowing that she didn't have much money left to live on, she was very excited.

Now Reba has always been the young lady to turn to for help. If she knew that you needed help, no matter what, she would be there. With a giving heart and soul, she always loved people. She always felt for her family and friends, and as long as she ate, they would eat as well. Over time though, she began to realize that people did not necessarily feel the same way about her and this broke both her heart and soul.

It was puzzling to Reba how she would do for others from her heart, but in her time of need, no one was there for her or her children. It broke her heart each day as she tried to reach out to others. Reba couldn't go to the interview because no one would watch Stacy for her. She had done all she could think of, even explaining that Stacy was a good girl. She's potty trained and she would even pack a big lunch for her just in case but knew she wouldn't be gone long; just to the interview and back.

All of the answers were, "No, I can't," or "Not today, maybe some other time!" Consequently, she didn't get the job.

Reba cried for days, her children would wipe her eyes and say, "Mommy, don't cry, we are going to be alright." They always knew the right thing to say to comfort each other; that's the way Reba was bringing them up, but each time, she looked in her cabinet, the food was getting low and so was her money. Not to mention, her clutch was going out on her car and she didn't feel safe driving it with her children in it.

Finally, Reba became desperate and knocked on the door of her neighbor across the hall. When she answered the door, Reba explained what she was going through, low food, and the lights were about to be cut off. Reba wasn't asking her for anything, just if she knew somewhere that she could get help for her and the children.

The lady was kind enough to say, "Yes, I have been noticing that it was just you and your children across the hall. I told my husband the other day that you were so quiet, we wouldn't have known you had children."

Reba smiled and said, "Thank you, ma'am. I try hard to raise my children the right way."

"I am off tomorrow," the lady said. Mrs. Marlene was her name. "I'll take you to see if you can get some food stamps and help with your lights," and she did just that. The first stop was food stamps.

Reba filled out the form and spoke with one of the social workers. "I am sorry," she said, "You have a newer model car and we can't help you unless you sell it. The value of your car is too much."

Confused, Reba said, "But it's not drivable and once I get it fixed, I have to find a job."

The social worker looked at Reba once again and said, "I am sorry, have a good day, maybe you can try again after you sell your car."

Walking out of the office, Mrs. Marlene knew that Reba had been turned down. "Reba," she said, "hold your head up, you're a good mother. Let's try one more place."

She took Reba to a church, through a back door, something she had never done before. There was a line on the inside, "Mrs. Marlene, why are we here?"

"Baby, they give out food for those who don't have."

Reba held her head down, thinking to herself. *How did I get here, my life is just a mess, HERE I GO AGAIN, just a mess if it's not one thing with me, it's another. My children, they didn't ask to be here, why should they have to live like this?*

Reba was feeling horrible, Stacy pulled her shirt for her to pick her up, and Reba held her all the way up the line.

It was Reba's turn and the lady asked, "How many in your household?"

Reba replied, "Four, my three children and myself."

The lady was putting extra things in her bag that none of the others were getting. She leaned toward Reba and spoke very softly, "I know you don't belong here, sweetheart, call home and go back. God has so much for you to do, this too shall pass."

Reba became numb she never saw this lady before but the way she was talking to her, it was as if she knew her. *Lord, is she an angel?*

Mrs. Marlene helped Reba and the baby get in the car and back home they went. They carried the bags up the stairs before the boys got home only to realize that her lights were out. "NO! NO!" Reba yelled out, "not now!" Here we go again; she was broke down and didn't know what else to do. *It never gets better was that what the lady was saying at the church?*

Reba's neighbor held in her arms and said, "It will be better. Tell you what I am going to do, Reba, I have a cooler that I am going to give you. I will keep it filled up with ice, and I will run a drop cord from my home into yours. The only thing is, when it's time for my husband to come home, I will have to unplug the cord. This has to stay between us, okay?"

"Yes, ma'am, thank you."

"It's going to be okay, baby, you will see."

That afternoon, her boys didn't notice that the lights were off or that they only had cold water. Reba had a microwave and she heated the water in that so they could all take a bath before the lights would go out, because Mrs. Marlene's husband would be home. It was hard on Reba seeing her children like this; she wanted so much to go home but she didn't even have enough money to call home. Her rent was due and she didn't have the money to pay it. Her only thoughts were, *all those I helped here, and no one remembered me.*

One day, she searched through all her bags and found five dollars' worth of change. Reba was at her lowest point, broke, and she tried to call home, but there was no answer. She tried again later that day, when the boys got home from school; but still no answer, so she took her change once again from the pay phone.

The kids didn't know any better. She took them to the playground not far from the office, and was praying the whole time that they wouldn't come and ask her for the rent now. She was two weeks late and still no notice had been placed on the door, as of yet.

That night, Reba and the kids ate crackers for dinner. That was all she had left. They drank water-there was no milk for the baby, and only a few Pampers were left. Reba put the babies to bed. They all slept together. She went in the front room looking out the window looking up into the sky; "Father, I know that you are real; you said in your word that you will never forsake us or leave us. In your word, you said all we have to do is ask, Lord I am ASKING; please help my children and me. We are hungry and have no help. I have no one left to turn to but you! Father, I tried to call home but there was no answer and I know that if I called on you, you would answer. I am scared, please send help right away!"

Reba got off her knees and went to bed, holding her child as tight as she could. Later that night, she heard a knock on the door and was scared to ask who it was. She tried to peek through the peephole but she couldn't tell who the people were. Her heart was racing, Reba thought to herself, *Father, please don't let them put us out, we have nowhere to go.* As she stood there, there was yet another knock. The kids were still asleep. Although Reba was so scared, tears began to run down her face, she could hear a soft voice inside saying, "Answer the door, your help is here."

Finally, she had the strength to say, "Who is it?"

"Reba, it's Mommy, baby, open the door."

And she did, it really was her mommy, and her baby sister, Mya. They all just held one another. But her sister was more concerned about her niece and nephews. "Reba, where are the kids?"

"They are sleeping, Mya."

"Turn the lights on so we can see."

"I can't, they are off, Mama. I'm sorry you had to see this."

"Reba, we came to get you and the kids. You don't have a choice this time either. You're coming home with us or we are taking the kids."

Reba looked at her mother and said, "Mommy, wait for me I am going to pack all that I can, but my car is not working."

Her mother asked, "Can you drive it at all?"

"Yes, but not far."

"Good, we will get it to a shop but you and these babies will not stay another night in the apartment like this."

Reba said, "Mom, I understand."

"What do you want to do with the furniture you have?"

"Can we just leave it? I don't want any more memories of this life."

"Are you sure? We can put it in storage and come back for it."

"Mom, I am sure."

Reba knocked on the neighbors' door and said, "Thank you for all you have done for me and my children, I am going back home."

Reba's mother, Regina, said, "Thank you for looking out for my daughter, I am truly grateful."

"Mrs. Marlene, I will not be taking any of my furniture, if you know of anyone who might be in need, as I was, will you make sure that get all they want before the office does whatever it is that they do?"

Mrs. Marlene gave Reba the biggest hug, "I am going to miss you sunshine, and you are always in my prayer. Y'all be safe on that road!"

# Chapter 8

# Life's too short

That very day, Reba's car was fixed, tuned up, and ready for the road trip back to New York. They made it back safe and sound, Reba was tired and worn out from the journey. She had become so depressed, she had lost a lot of weight, not having much to eat, worrying about her children, and people talking about her, but no one would reach out to help her. One thing Reba did learn out of this lesson is that life is too short and we only have one life to live.

She felt that it was okay to love, just guard your heart in the process and that everyone is not like her; but she had to learn that the hard way. Days went by, Regina gave Reba some time to rest and get herself together.

One day when they were sitting together in the living room, Regina asked, "Reba, are you okay?"

"Yes, Mom, I am better now that I am home."

"No, Reba, are you really okay?"

"Yes, Mommy, why are you looking at me like that and asking me that question?"

"I am going to be honest with you. I got a call from down there saying that you were on drugs and that you're looking real bad."

"OH MY GOD, Mommy that's a lie. I have never smoked any drugs; Lord knows I am telling the truth. Mommy, please believe me. I lost the weight because I was so stressed, lonely, scared, and couldn't eat."

Reba began to tell her mother about everything that happened while she was in Columbia and her mother understood why her child was looking the way she was.

Regina cried, "Baby, you've been through so much at such a young age, it's time to get your life right with GOD."

"Mom, I prayed the night you came and asked him to send help right away and you were at my door that very night. Mom, we didn't have any more food and I was scared."

Regina couldn't believe all that had happened, "No one would help you?" Her mother shook her head in disbelief that her child had been through this all this alone. Her mother had always been a praying woman, giving her life to the Lord many years ago. "Reba don't hold grudges, keep your head up baby, it's going to be alright. Just pray on it and ask the Lord to release you from all the pain and disappointment that you have been through and he will work it all out. Reba you're home, in the morning, let's get the kids registered in school, and move forward."

The next morning, Reba did just that, the kids would be starting school in a couple weeks and summer was almost over. She sat at the table watching Troy and her youngest brother BJ play in the back yard, while Isaiah met his own new friend, Joey. Stacy, the little one, was running around the house playing with her dolls, just as happy as she could be.

Reba asked her mother about Charles. "Mom, have you seen him at all since I've been gone?"

"Yes, he looks the same."

"That's good," she replied.

"Reba," said Mom, "he called when I had my phone on at the house in South Carolina and ask if he could see the kids and when were we coming back. Do you think I should let him know we are back?

"Reba, I can't answer that for you, pray on it."

"Okay, Mom, I will."

She did just that; but did she wait for an answer? No, she did not. Reba took the kids over to see Charles. He was still living with his mother in a one-bedroom apartment. He slept on the couch in the front room. The house was so cluttered with things it was senseless, but that was their house and Reba never said a word.

When they arrived, he gave Reba a big hug and the same with the kids. He made them lunch. The kids were so excited to see him. It was a pleasant afternoon until his mother came home.

"Oh, you're back in town," she said.

Reba just gave her a look like, *lady not today, please.*

Charles didn't like her comment either, "Ma, chill," he said.

She gave him a look, cut her eyes, walked in her room, and slammed the door.

At that point, Reba was ready to go, "Charles, I just

wanted to let you know that we were back in town; here's my mother's number. Thanks for the lunch today. The kids and I enjoyed hanging out with you, talk to you soon."

Reba still had love for him but she knew that she would never go backwards with any of her broken relationships. That was her rule, and it seemed to work for her.

She found a job soon after moving back. Although things were looking up for her, something still wasn't feeling right. Each day, she had to pass her father's burial ground, which was tough emotionally. Reba's sisters were all married now and they were all doing well.

One day Reba sat her mother down, "Mom, I don't want to stay in New York, it's just not for me, all my sisters are married and gone, it's just us and the kids here; let's move to Atlanta."

Reba talked to her sister, Ann, and her baby sister, Mya, both living there with their families; they were happy that their big sister and mother were planning to relocate there too. Regina had clearly agreed with her daughter, "It's time to move on, life is too short."

Reba's other sister, Deborah, was living with her husband in New Jersey and they were not quite ready to move south. Reba and her mother were disappointed that they were not ready to leave the North but they understood.

Reba had it all planed out, they made a trip to Atlanta and stayed a week with Ann and her family. Ann took time out with them each day, showing them around town until they found an apartment. It was a very nice three-bedroom, with two full baths, and they even had central air.

*My Life Story*

Reba and her mother couldn't believe the price, even with the central air, it was nothing compared to the price they were paying in New York.

After finding their new home, back up North they went, the kids had two more weeks before school was out and they were sad to be leaving their friends. They knew that they were not coming back. Nevertheless, Reba and her mother knew that this was the best move they could make for the kids; New York was getting too rough. The time had come, the Mayflower Moving Company pulled up and the loading had begun, Reba was so excited and so was her mother. They looked at each other, *a new beginning.*

The kids were sitting on the side with their friends, looking sad and lost. Reba went and sat beside them, hugging all their friends, telling them, "Once we get settled, I promise, they will call you all the time and you can even come down to visit as much as you want."

Then the kids all had big smiles on their faces and were happy knowing that their friends wouldn't be forgotten. All the hugs were given; he cars were loaded, Reba and her mother were off on the road: *Highway 95, here we come.*

Both cars were rolling-Reba had the two little ones with her; Troy, her mom, and her baby brother were in the other car. It was a very long journey but they made it; They pulled up to the new apartment, got the keys, and went off to their building. The kids were excited to finally get out of the cars. They went running upstairs into the apartment, so happy, "This room is mine," they were yelling, "no my room."

Reba and her mother would just laugh with the joy they both felt at a new start, a new beginning, as they unloaded all that they had packed from the cars. Finding the Publix grocery store around the corner was wonderful; then there was shopping and getting ready for the furniture to come. They slept on the floor the first two nights, waiting for the truck, which was still a no show on the third day, but the truck finally pulled up and all was well.

Reba's sisters and their families all came over, and they all had a good time. It was the summer and although it wasn't time for school yet, the time was near. Reba found a job at a Honda car dealership, long hours, and just about seven days a week. Not selling many cars, she knew that she had to find a new job and her thoughts went back to school, *it's now time for a career.*

With the summer over, the kids were now in school all day, including little Stacy, and she was so happy, on her big day, on the big yellow school bus. Reba stood there and watched her baby girl as she went off for her first day of school; she even shed a tear, what a proud mother she was.

She had the day off from the dealership and she wanted to take it to just relax and think. I am almost twenty-eight years old, what have I accomplished in my life but heartbreak after heartbreak. She grabbed her Bible and began to read, she felt like she needed to start in the New Testament, so she started with John 1: "In the beginning was the word, and the word was with God, and the word was God."

Reading this, Reba was starting to feel in her heart

that even though she had been through so much, she felt like the Lord had been with her through all her storms, even though she never understood why there were so many.

# Chapter 9

# A Liar and a Cheat

Another year had gone by and Reba was very focused on her life and her children. She had found a church where she and the family had been attending and growing in the Lord. Finally, at peace with herself, although she was still working at the Honda dealership, she decided she had enough and she was going to move on by faith.

After searching for some time, Reba was hired to sell perfume for a company that promised her an office of her own. This was new for her, but she felt, *if I can sell cars this should be a piece of cake,* or so she thought. Reba worked with another young lady, Kim, who was hired at the same time, and they both decided to work the West End side of town.

One summer day, Reba and Kim were working their area, doing pretty well for themselves, although they had good days and bad days. That day, Reba heard someone call her name; it was an old classmate of hers from the Valley in New York.

"Mitchell," she said, "what are you doing in Atlanta?"

He smiled and gave her a huge hug, "I am living

here now. I've been here about three months now. Girl, what are you doing out here?"

"Trying to sell some cologne," she laughed, "just trying something new."

"What do you have?"

Reba was happy. He brought three different colognes from her, and that was the only sale she made for the day. She was also happy to see someone that she knew in this town. Mitchell and Reba exchanged numbers; they talked that evening and did a lot of catching up with one another. She never knew what had happened to him in high school, she had asked others what happened too, but no one knew. They stayed in touch and decided to get together and go out for lunch three weeks later.

They had lunch at the Cheesecake Factory, one of Reba's favorite places to eat. Looking beautiful, she was ready for her first date in Atlanta and, she was excited to see Mitchell. When she got there, he was waiting patiently for her and they were seated.

"So, Reba, what have you been up to it's been some years?"

"Yea it has, Mitchell. Wow where do I begin I have three beautiful children, two boys and a girl. My oldest son, Troy, is twelve. Isaiah is eight, and my baby girl, Stacy, is four. Married once, which didn't last long. My dad passed but Mom is doing well and I am living my life one day at a time. What about you Mitchell?"

"Married once, two children Christen and Mitchell Jr., they both are living in New York with their mother. My mom passed and my dad is doing well."

"How about your siblings?" Reba asked, knowing them all.

"Everyone is okay," he replied.

Their food was served. "Mitchell, I must ask, what happened to you in school? It was like you disappeared."

"Reba, I won't lie, my life was a mess. I started running with the wrong people. I was in and out of jail, even got caught up on drugs."

Her eyes got big; she couldn't even swallow her food. She sat back in the seat and just stared at him, *like not again.*

"Reba, why are you looking at me like that?"

"Well, I must be honest too. I have been through enough dating addicts and I just can't do that anymore in my life! I've been through so much of that that, there was a rumor in my family that I was using. I just don't want to go through that feeling ever again."

"Reba, I have been clean for ten years. I make meeting faithfully, and I have a sponsor. That was why I left the Valley, I wanted to stay clean."

"I hear that," she said.

"Reba, thank you for having lunch with me. There's nothing like having lunch with an old friend."

"You're welcome," she replied, "I must admit I had a great time."

Mitchell walked her to her car. They hugged and off she went. Her mind was racing, she even started talking to herself, "Now, Reba, I don't care how good he looks, he was once on drugs, you made a promise to yourself that you were not going through no more drama." She took a deep breath and decided not to take any more of his calls.

A month had passed and Mitchell never gave up on trying to see her again. The phone rang and her son, Troy, answered, "Mommy, you have a phone call."

Reba looked at the phone and it was Mitchell. The look she gave Troy made him take off into his room and he stayed there until the coast was clear. "Hi, Mitchell."

"Reba, where have you been? I have been calling you."

"Yes, I know, I've just been so busy."

"I understand," he replied. "Hey, I am in Jonesboro, I remember you said you lived out this way, are you busy?"

Reba was shaking the phone from her ears, putting it back to her ears. "No, you can come by." She gave him the address, her mom and the kids were all home so she felt like it would be okay.

Thirty minutes later, the doorbell rang. Her mother answered the door, "Come on in, so you're Mitchell. Reba told me about you, the two of you were classmates."

"Yes, ma'am," he replied.

Reba entered the room, "Hi, Mitchell, have a seat."

Mitchell stayed and they all laughed and talked for quite some time. He even stayed over for dinner. All the kids really liked him and he seemed to have enjoyed them as well. By then, it was getting late so Reba walked him to her front porch.

"I really enjoyed your company," she said. "Thank you for thinking of me when you were in the area."

*My Life Story*

"It was my pleasure. Thank you for having me."

She gave him a hug and off he went. When she went back into the house, her mom was still sitting in the living room. "Reba, he seems to be a nice guy."

"Yes, Mom, he does, but that's how they all seem to start out and I'm just not ready to go through that again anytime soon!"

Her mother laughed, "I understand, baby, take your time."

"That's my plan," Reba replied, "good night."

"Good night, baby."

Mitchell had been calling Reba every day. Some days she would take his calls and some days she wouldn't. She had really started breaking down though and her heart started to soften for him. Finally, she decided, *Okay he seems to be a straight up guy, it's been a little over a year not being in a relationship or seeing anyone. Let me give him a try, but I am truly going to take it one day at a time*, and she told Mitchell just that.

The two of them starting dating more. He would come around her home and it was as if they were becoming one big family. After two years of dating, they decided to move in together. Mitchell would go to recovery meetings and Reba would join him often. She had always been the type of person to support others who were trying to move ahead.

Reba was starting to fall in love with Mitchell. He was good to her, but deep in her heart, she felt like she could never find the love that Charles had given her. In her eyes,

Charles was really her true love. Mitchell was working for a trash company, pulling trash each day, making okay money, but he was a very good provider in their home and Reba really liked that he knew how to handle his business, with everything paid on time.

Saturday mornings would come and Mitchell would not miss his meeting. One day, while they were at one of his meetings, Reba noticed that he was watching another woman walking around the room, brown skinned, nice long hair, and a neat shapely body, very friendly. At times, *a little too friendly*, Reba thought.

Reba always attended these meetings with him; in fact, it was almost becoming a normal thing for her to do. Although at first, she felt out of place, now there were times when she wished that she too could share, but Reba was not a recovering addict.

Mitchell was changing now that he began to meet more people in his meetings; some of them would meet and go to different meetings, these meetings would be for recovery only. Reba was fine with what he was doing; it freed her time up on some Saturdays to hang out with the kids or to have free time for herself.

Another year went by and Reba decided to move out of the apartment. She found a nice three-bedroom town house, three levels; it was perfect, plenty of space.

They were all settled in and Mitchell was changing day-by-day. When his phone rang, he would take his calls in another room, or outside. She never said one word, but she watched closely.

Mitchell came home one day, "Reba, listen, I don't know why Troy thinks he is so grown, but I tell you what, in this house, he will not hang out when he wants to and come in all times of night! And I mean that."

It was as if Mitchell was a wild man. Reba jumped, never having seen him act like this before, "Mitchell, are you okay?" She asked.

"I am fine; did you hear what I just said to you?"

Reba replied, "Wait a minute, Troy does not hang out at all times of the night. Where are you getting this from? Just because when you get home he's not in the house at five in the afternoon doesn't mean he is out there hanging out all night. The kids get home and do their chores and homework and then they go outside. Why should I make them stay in the house? They know what time to be home and they have never missed a curfew, unless they call and ask."

*What was really his problem?* Reba was beginning wonder and she got upset. *What does he really have going on in his life, late night calls, and all these meetings? Lord, not again, this one here needs not to go there when it comes to my kids!*

Reba decided to go back to school and take up some medical courses and so she did, finishing up with awards, and feeling great, she landed a wonderful job in a doctor's office in College Park, Georgia.

The office was small, with one doctor, a front office staff, and two medical assistants; Reba was one of them. Still hanging in the relationship with Mitchell, things in the house were starting to get worse. Troy and Mitchell weren't getting along at all and Reba didn't like that one bit, it was almost as if Troy reminded Mitchell of himself, *but why?* Reba couldn't understand it.

Finally, Troy came to his mother one day and said, "Mom, I don't know why Mitchell doesn't like me, but I can't take it anymore. He is not my father and he's not going to be tripping on me like he is crazy every time he sees me. I can be watching TV and he will come in my room looking for something to fuss about. Mom, that's why I stay out until it's time for me to come home, his mouth, he always cussing at me like I am grown."

Reba was in shock, because she had no clue what was going on in her own home. Troy had always been the laid back one of her children, he was quiet and always did what he was supposed to do. Reba started to get very angry and couldn't wait for Mitchell to walk through that door! It was getting later and later, here he comes walking in the door, and she was standing right there.

"What's your problem?" He asked.

"What's my problem? You're the problem, why are you having a hard time with my son, Troy, and who gave you the right to use all kinds of language to a child?"

"Reba, let me tell you something, he is now sixteen years old, and he's not a child."

"Really, is that what your parents used to tell you when you were that age? Because in my book, they are still children, until they turn eighteen, reality is, then they are still not ready, the bottom line is, Mitchell if I ever find out that you are talking to any of my children like that again, there will be some real problems and I MEAN THAT!" Reba gave him a look and walked off.

Mitchell stood there and looked crazy; the house was quiet for a while. The tension in the house was thick and Reba did not care, she was waiting for him to slip up again with her child. While never apologizing, Mitchell knew that Reba wasn't playing, and one day he came to her saying, "Listen, I really want this to work for us, Reba, and I need you."

Reba believed that he was sincere, but he was a slick talker, and she knew that something had changed in their relationship. Nonetheless, feeling this one might be better because he was a clean addict and had been for years, she tried to make it work.

The holidays would come and Reba always wanted to make her children happy, Mitchell, still working, pulling trash, and acting funny, it finally got to a point that Reba felt like, *Right now, until I am able to make my move, it's all about my kids.*

Christmas morning, she had been saving all year long, and she had her mother and her younger brother come over to enjoy Christmas with them. The tree was as tall as the ceiling in the house and full of light; this year, gifts were all over the room, because they all wouldn't fit under the tree. Reba truly went all out to make her children happy. Although Mitchell didn't offer one dime toward the kids' gifts, he was playing the daddy role and Reba still put his name on all the gifts, knowing he didn't give her any help in purchasing them. Because she loved him and wanted a family so much, she did whatever she could to make it seem like they were just that, a family, a happy family.

Everyone was pleased and that Christmas, Mitchell proposed to her. She was so excited and she said yes! Even though she knew there were things going on behind closed doors, it was a still happy moment in her life. Reba felt like if they were to marry, *maybe he could change, after all he isn't on drugs, he's a hard worker and a good provider.*

A few months after Christmas, her mother moved in with them and Reba was very happy to have her and her younger brother in her home. Soon after that, Mitchell and Reba decided to get married in the mountains, Pigeon Forge, Tennessee, without family or friends.

It was just the two of them; they decided to rent a cabin and that's where they got married. The grounds had a minster on site they had a small cake. Reba wore a beautiful cream-colored semi-gown and Mitchell had on a nice double-breasted suit, which she had bought for him. It was a happy day for them both, peaceful, with snow falling down and the fireplace in the cabin was blazing. It was very romantic and after the ceremony, they both agreed to love one another forever.

They stayed four days, enjoying the sights, shopping, restaurants and so much more. When it came time to go back home, he held her hand all the way back to Georgia. When they arrived home, all the kids were there. They made little banners for the front door and it was beautiful to see them standing there, all but Troy.

"Mom, where's Troy?" Reba asked.

"He's outside, honey."

Reba's heart sank because she knew why he wasn't there and she understood. Reba loved her children but she felt like she had to have a life too. She waited for him to come home and he did before his time. "Hey, son, how are you, baby?"

Troy gave his mom the best hug and said, "Mom, I love you, sorry I wasn't home for you when you got back."

Reba looked at him and said, "Shhhhh, it's okay, I LOVE YOU MORE SON AND DON'T YOU EVER FORGET THAT!"

They hugged each other tighter and smiled. A year had gone by now, the neighborhood seemed to be going down, and Reba felt like it was time to move on from this area. Her mother found a nice place for her and BJ. Regina was happy to be moving into her own place but Reba was sad because she didn't want her mother out of her eyesight, ever again.

Nonetheless, Reba's mom moved and was all settled in and enjoying her new home. Meanwhile, Reba took the kids out and starting looking around at some new homes and new subdivisions past the Morrow Area. One day she found a home in Chad Landing a new subdivision, and the homes were beautiful. The kids loved it and so did Reba. Now the challenge was to get Mitchell to feel the same way.

Saturday afternoon, when he came in after his meeting, Reba thought it would be the perfect time to tell him all about the property she had found. He listened and decided to take a look at what she was so excited about.

The sales office was open; the model is what she was wanting: five bedrooms, three full bathrooms, large garages, and plenty of land. The inside of the house was very large with a beautiful fireplace.

Mitchell agreed to move forward with the process and all the paper work was going well. They were approved, but only in Mitchell's name. Reba didn't have enough credit established to go on the contract. She was very disappointed but determined to fix her credit, and in a hurry.

Each day, when Reba got off work, she would go out to the site and take pictures, as their home was being built. It was so exciting for her and the kids. She was to the point with Mitchell that she let him go to his meetings and do whatever it took to stay clean.

Months had passed and it was move in day, all was well, new furniture was coming, the kids were all happy; they all had their own rooms. Reba had the kids so spoiled, they each had their own computer in their own room, and they shared their own phone line. Reba's main thing was to keep your grades up in school or Mommy will not be spoiling you, and they knew that she meant just that.

After moving into their home, Mitchell decided to leave the trash company, since he wanted to go back to school for computers. His plan was to work part-time and go to school full-time.

Reba was okay with that, she was able to make the mortgage, and she felt that he had helped her while she went to school full-time. Many nights, she would stay up with him studying, helping him prepare for his tests, or helping him break a computer down and rebuild it.

At this point, things were going well. Mitchell was focused on his new career, and Reba was proud of him. One year later, he completed his course, on the honor roll, and was ready to start his new career. He went for an interview at a well-known computer company and he got the job, making double the amount of money he was making before.

Reba was proud of him, and praying that because she had stayed up with him so many nights, giving her support, helping him pass all his tests, and helping him by being by his side through school, things might change, and there may be hope in their marriage.

Things were going well for a while, but a year or so later, Mitchell had started back with his old ways, and this time it had gotten worst.

Reba came home one day and noticed that things in Troy's room were missing, and so was he! "Mitchell, where is Troy, and why aren't his things in his room?"

"I told him that he will not disrespect me and this is my house and he had a choice, to either get his sh*t together, or get out of my house. So he decided to get out, and when he left, I told him that he is never welcome back in my home again and if you have something to say about it, you can take your kids and leave too."

Reba was angry and devastated that he would put her child out like that. She had always wondered why he disliked her son so much. Reba found Troy; he was with her mother and younger brother. She sat down with him in private and asked, "Son, what happened?"

"Mom, I am never going back there, ever since I was younger, he would always accuse me of doing something that I was not doing. If it wasn't selling drugs, it was me being on drugs, or talking to me any kind of way. I could be watching TV, Ma, and he would just go off on me."

Regina was not happy that her grandson was still going through this.

Reba asked her mother if she knew this was going on and she said yes.

"Mom, why didn't you tell me?"

"I did, but you didn't want to hear it, or it was always I'll take care of it."

Reba held her son and said, "Troy, Mom always told you that I wouldn't let anything happen to you and Mom loves you more than you could ever imagine. That's you, and your brother and sister. Son, trouble don't last always, are you okay staying here with Grandma?"

"Yes."

"Mom, is it okay for him to stay with you and BJ?"

"Yes." Her mother replied.

Troy looked at his mom with the most heartbroken look, "Okay, but Troy please don't give Grandma a hard time."

"Mom, you both know that I am only a phone call away."

Reba cried all the way back home; she was devastated that her son was not with them. This was the first time that they had ever been separated. Reba knew something had to be done. Mitchell always had a little cockiness to himself, but when she got home, she really let him have it. She was to the point in her life that she felt that the Lord would fight this battle.

Their argument was nasty. He even tried to put her and the other two kids out, but she told him, "I wish you might," Reba said. "I was the one to put the deposit down, I am the one who chose the layout, and had the modeling done in this house. All you did was run the streets, doing only God knows what."

Mitchell saw the look on her face, then backed off real quick, and left the house.

Reba cried many days and nights, feeling the loneliness again, not having her oldest son with her, and trying to maintain everything as a mother.

Life in that house was hell; Mitchell would come home every other night saying that he had to work late.

She knew that was not the truth, but in her heart, Reba was broken all over again, *not another woman,* was all she kept thinking. She felt like because he remained clean in his sobriety, what else would it be?

Although Reba was to the point where she didn't want him to touch her, she still wanted her marriage to work. She would cook and iron his clothing, or put them in the cleaners. The house was always clean, but nothing seemed to make him happy.

Plenty of days, Stacy and Isaiah would hear their mother in her room crying, and they would say, "Mom, please don't cry, it's going to be okay, we promise. Isn't that what you would tell us when we were little?"

"Yes, baby, I sure did."

One day, Reba got a call and it was Charles' mother telling her that he had a stroke. Reba lost it; she didn't know how to tell her baby girl that her daddy was very ill. Reba asked, "What hospital is he in, how is he doing?"

His mother didn't want to give her much information at all, so Reba just asked her to keep her posted on his condition. She didn't know how she got her phone number, but it didn't matter, her true love was very ill. Stacy came home and Reba sat her down and told her that her dad was very ill and she was going to try her very best to get her up there to see him.

Mitchell came home later that evening, Reba had told him what had happened earlier that day, and he looked at her and asked, "Well, what do you want me to do?"

Reba replied in a humble way, "Mitchell, I don't want you to do anything. I would like to take Stacy home to see her father."

"You're not going anywhere, do you hear me?"

His tone brought back flashes of Braxton, but his look was even more frightening. "Mitchell, please that's her father, tomorrow is not promised to any of us."

"I said no."

Reba just walked away and got in bed, balled up in the fetal position, and cried. Mitchell had become very verbally abusive toward her; one day he told her that the only thing she was good for was being on her back every night. He took all of her credit cards and tore them up; things went completely downhill in their marriage.

One evening, the kids all went to their grandmother's for a night. Reba wanted to try something different; maybe Mitchell would just give her a chance. She had her hair done that day and bought a beautiful cream-colored lingerie gown; she lit candles throughout the house and cooked a special dinner. It was getting late and no Mitchell, until she finally heard one of the garage doors go up. She became excited, but nervous at the same time, the house smelled good, and she waited for him to reach the top of the wide stairs in their home. She could hear him come through the garage door, entering the house.

"What the hell is all this," he said, as he got to the top of the stairs. "What are you standing there looking like that for? You need to go put some clothes on. I don't want none of that," he said, as he walked into the room.

Reba was numb. One-by-one, she started blowing the candles out, starting at the fireplace, she went all through the house, even to the bottom of the stairs. When she looked up, he was headed back out of the house with his overnight bag.

Not able to move from the top of the stairs, she cried her heart out. Reba had done so much for Mitchell, she helped him through his schooling, and he had his degrees in computer, making good money now, more than he ever did. Reba never asked him for anything because she was the type of women who always had her own; all she ever wanted was to be loved.

Time went on, and she wouldn't even hold a conversion with him. Then one day, Reba went to her door and there was a package. She sat down and opened it; it had clothing in it that looked so familiar. She screamed from the top of her lungs; it was Charles, he had passed. His mother sent his obituary with a few of his clothes, a cap, and some pictures that Reba had given him of her and the kids.

Charles' mother had never called her back to tell

her anything; when she had tried to call, no one would answer the phone, but once and Charles could barely talk. He did try his best, asking Reba when she was bringing Stacy. All she could do was cry, because she didn't want to be beaten any more in her life.

Stacy and Mitchell came in the house at the same time and Stacy ran to her mother, "Mommy, what's wrong?"

Mitchell just stood there and looked, "It's your daddy baby. He has passed away."

Stacy screamed and cried. She fell into her mother's arms and they cried together. Mitchell tried to pull Stacy into his arms but she did not let go of her mother. Reba looked at him with the most evil look, one that simultaneously said get away from my child and I will hate you for the rest of my life.

Mitchell left the room and gave them time with one another, months went by, and the house was extremely quiet. Mitchell would try to talk to Isaiah and Stacy. They both would give him a look and did what he would ask of them, but otherwise, they would never say a word to him.

There were plenty of nights when Reba would go and sit on her pouch, look up at the beautiful stars and pray, asking the Lord to set her free from this nightmare, "Lord, I have done all that I can as a wife to make this work. I am tired. In your words, a wife is to be submissive to her husband and I have done it all. Father, show me that it's okay for me to leave and I shall promise to never look back."

The signs came faster that she could have ever asked. One bright morning, something woke Reba up and she looked at Mitchell, the light was shining brightly down on him, as he slept. She looked at him closely. He had hickeys all over his body, from his neck to the bottom of his thighs.

Reba screamed, "Mitchell, how could you, and why? Why?"

Mitchell woke up out of his sleep and began to yell back at her, saying, "Now you found what you were looking for, I hope you are happy, because I am."

"So you know," Reba replied, "I knew all the time, Mitchell, but I didn't want to believe it. The old saying is true, what goes on in the dark always come to the light," she began to praise God right there before him.

"There you go again, you and your GOD!"

"YES," she retorted, "YOU WILL REAP WHAT YOU SOW!"

Now Reba has her answer and she knew it was time to go. Isaiah wasn't feeling well one day and he stayed home from school. He called Reba at work and said, "Mom, who's this lady Mitchell is bringing in our house?"

"What lady?"

"Mom, she has long hair and she light skinned."

"I am on my way," Reba replied.

Isaiah said, "No, Mom, I got this one."

Mitchell walked up the stairs laughing, had his arms around the lady's waist. When he looked up, he was shocked to see Isaiah home from school.

"Mitchell, who is this lady you are bringing in my momma's house?"

Mitchell was speechless and asked her to wait in the car. Then he replied, "It's just a friend of mine from my job."

As he walked past him, Isaiah said, "Well, Mom's on her way home and you tell her that one!" Isaiah was angry; he walked in his room and closed the door.

Reba couldn't get there fast enough. Mitchell took off when he heard she was on her way home. Reba walked in and called out to Isaiah, "Where is he at?"

"Mom, they left."

Reba said, "That's it, we must look even harder to get out of this house!" Every day, the three of them searched for an apartment. She had already been turned down so many times, since she didn't have enough rental history on her credit. Although it became very depressing for her, Reba would always find her prayer place at night on her pouch. Looking up, she prayed, "Lord, I know you didn't bring me this far to leave us, you said you will make a way. Help me and my children get out of this house please, Lord."

And so he did. Not giving up, that Saturday, Reba and the kids went to three different places, and she finally found one. It was an apartment and it was gated. Reba went inside and there stood one of the managers she had known from the town house, "Reba how are you, sweetheart?"

Reba broke down and cried, because she knew her problems were over. She began to tell her what was going on with her and Mitchell and the manager became very angry. "Wow, he always made it seem like you two were doing just fine, he sure had me fooled."

"Yes, ma'am, you, and many others, when we were in the public's eye.

"Reba, I know how it is to be in a battered relationship. I once was there too. I am going to give you this two bedroom apartment, you and those babies get out of there."

Reba signed her lease. She and the kids were so excited. Then she explained to them, "Now, what I want is for the two of you to go through all of your things and what you don't want, get rid of it, and start packing, but keep everything out of sight until I tell you."

Reba had the apartment for a week, moving things in slowly. Mitchell was so busy doing his own thing; he didn't realize that she had already started moving things out of the home that she had bought. One evening, the house phone rang and Reba answered it, "Hello," the voice of a women spoke, asking for Mitchell. "He's not home, this is his wife. May I take a message?"

"Yes, you sure can. He should be on his way there, once he gets there, tell him that Tracy called and said his dinner is ready and don't take too long!"

Reba said, "Excuse me, would you repeat that."

"That's right, you heard me the first time. I said his dinner is ready."

Reba replied, "Girl, you know he is a married man?"

"Yes, I do, and I've been all through your house." Then she began to tell Reba what her house looked like, including her bedroom.

Reba fell to her knees and yelled, "My God, what has he done?" Then she continued, "Young lady, you shall reap what you sow in the word of God, you shall."

"Let me tell something, I am a woman of God, and I know his word."

Reba retorted, "Look you Jezebel, if you really knew God's word, you would not be doing the things you're doing! You shall reap what you sow, and it will come back on you! If not you, it may come back on your daughter."

"Who told you I have a daughter?"

Reba replied, "My GOD, don't lie! If I was you," Reba said, "listen closely, all I am saying to you, sweetheart, is that I can tell you about the price you will surely pay. I know because I am reaping it now, since I was once in your shoes, years ago. Funny, now you're the other woman, just as I was many years ago. The God I chose to serve is a forgiving god and he will forgive you as he forgave me, it's not too late." Reba told her, "I shall keep you and your child in my prayers."

Tracy replied, "He said you were crazy."

"Yes, ma'am. I am crazy for Jesus because he is my savior!"

Tracy hung up and never called her home again. Mitchell came in the house thirty minutes later and Reba was ready.

He stood at the door, seeing the way she was looking at him, he asked, "What's wrong with you?"

Indeed, Reba was looking at him as if he was the nastiest man who walked the earth. She replied, "Your girl Tracy called. She said that dinner was ready and don't take too long to get there."

His mouth dropped in disbelief.

Reba said, "Close your mouth, Mitchell; it's all in the open now. I really got the message. I have made up my mind, I am not going to question you, and I am not going to waste my energy."

Mitchell tried to explain.

She put her finger to her mouth and said, "Hush, you two will reap what you sow. It's all good, baby, just remember I tried and did all I could as a wife. Mitchell I loved you and I put you before my children and my God. NO MORE! I give GOD the praise for bringing me back to my right mind."

As she walked away, in her soft voice, saying, "Don't be late, after all your dinner will get cold."

Mitchell came up the stairs, looking behind him, not knowing what Reba really had planned. She sat in front of her fireplace and watched the television that sat over it. She could hear Mitchell on the phone in the bedroom. It didn't faze her, as she knew that this was her last weekend in this house. Mitchell stayed home that night and he kept trying to talk to Reba; but she paid him no attention and slept in Troy's room instead.

The week passed and it was Friday morning, still saying few words to very little to Mitchell.

"Reba, you're not going to work today?"

She answered, "No, not today, Mitchell, why did you ask?"

His reply was, "I am asking you because you don't normally take time off."

"Why do you care? You haven't all year long."

"Reba, I am truly sorry."

"Yes, Mitchell, I must agree, but just remember, you said it, not me!"

Reba had her plan in place for that morning and

she waited for him to leave. Then she called him at work and told him that she was going to do a little shopping.

"Reba."

"Yes, Mitchell, I really do love you," she said "okay," and hung up the phone. Then, dialing right back out, she called her brother-in-law. Reba had already paid for a U-Haul and her boys and their friends were waiting right around the corner to start moving.

Then they all came in with the truck. There were ten of them total, moving everything that Reba had bought, leaving the one chair that was in his name. Reba was tired of Mitchell and the things that he put had her through. She took all the food, can goods, dishware, and silverware; she even dumped the ice and left one roll of toilet paper in the middle of the floor with a letter that said, "Mitchell thank you for all the hell you put me through. Now I am a stronger woman, know that God was with me through this storm, and now I stand. This roll is for you to wipe your behind, just like you used to give me yours to kiss… you're free now!"

Reba looked at the house once again, for the very last time, and said, "Father, I will not look back," and she didn't, as she pulled off.

Reba had taken Isaiah and Stacy out of the school they were attending and they started at a new one. She knew that Mitchell would try to get back at her by getting to the kids, but she was a step ahead of him on that.

Her family was prepared for him and they called her saying, "Mitchell is driving by looking to see if your car or the kids were out here playing."

Reba asked, "Did he stop?"

"No, he is just driving by."

Then Mitchell started calling her cell phone, leaving messages, "When I find you and your kids, I am going to kill you all."

Reba was not afraid at all, these calls from him went on for a week. He even continued driving past her family's home, but never stopping.

One day, he called Reba's phone, this time the message was different, "Reba, I never meant to hurt you. Please come home, I really need you. Please forgive me, call me back."

Reba's heart was saddened to hear Mitchell sound like he was in so much pain and she felt what he was saying, but she made a promise to never look back and she didn't. Finally, though, she took his call and he burst out in tears.

"Reba, please come home, I'm so lonely without you."

Reba had tears running out her eyes, but she said, "Mitchell, I can't, my heart says yes, but my soul says no. For years I followed my heart and not my soul and I can't do it any longer, it's now time for me to get my life in order, not with man, but with my God. I wish you well, my friend."

"Reba, I understand I lost out."

"Yes, Mitchell, you have, I truly wish you God's blessing, but no more. I went through so many storms, yet I stand, and that's only by the grace of God, but now I understand why. Goodbye, Mitchell."

"Goodbye, Reba."

She didn't hear from him for two months and then one day she got a phone call and it was him.

"Hi, Mitchell, how are you?" Reba asked.

"I am good," he replied, "Reba, I just wanted you to know before you hear it in the streets; I filed for our divorce."

"Okay, that's fine."

"Reba, as soon as the divorce is final, I will be getting married and we have plans to get married in the mountains."

Reba didn't know what to say. "Mitchell, you are really taking her to the mountains that you and I got married in?"

"Yes."

"Wow," she replied. "Mitchell, tell me is this the same one that you had in our home and who put all those hickeys on you?"

"No, this is someone else, she was all about money."

Reba's mouth dropped. "Thank you, Lord," she said on the phone, "Father, I thank you for removing things in my life and making arrangements so I can't turn around."

Mitchell was quiet on the phone after her praise. Reba said, "Mitchell, I wish you the best."

The papers came in and Reba called Mitchell's lawyer, asking if he knew that Mitchell had cheated on her by committing adultery. His attorney was shocked saying, "No, he didn't tell me that."

Reba replied, "Well, that's Mitchell, he's a liar and a cheat. I just wanted to make sure that these papers were legit. I will be signing them and putting them in the mail today."

Reba did just that, and never heard from Mitchell again. Life for Reba has been good ever since. Learning new things each day, finding out that things are not what they seem to be, and that includes her surroundings. A few new things have come about and Reba can't wait to share them with you.

World, lookout. Reba is going to really have you thinking on a whole different level! People are strange, they will have you thinking that something is wrong with you, but the question really should be, *When was the last time you looked in the mirror?*

**THERE IS SO MUCH MORE REBA IS ABOUT TO LEARN IN HER LIFE AND THAT IT'S OK TO BE A SINGLE MOTHER! KEEP YOUR EARS AND EYES OPEN, SHE WILL BE BACK!**

# Epilogue

Reba's life is like the life of a butterfly. She has gone through many trials and tribulations. One day she sat down and decided to analyze her life. She began to realize that much like a butterfly going through metamorphosis; she had to experience much heartache to blossom into the beautiful woman of God that she is today.

Think about it, a butterfly starts off as a caterpillar, this is the time in your life when everything seems to move slow and many of the people around you just seem to walk all over you, much like the people in Reba's life did to her. It's in this early stage when they tend to take advantage of your kindness, looking at it as if it were some sort of a weakness. The next step in the life of a butterfly is what we refer to as metamorphosis. It's during this period when we should sit back and reevaluate our lives. This stage is where we begin to think of ways to make our situation or surroundings better. Not necessarily dwelling on the past anymore, because you are no longer a victim. Sometimes we all have to take a good look in the mirror and remind ourselves "I AM SOMEBODY." Reba now looks in the mirror every day and she tells herself just that. Every morning she tells herself, *I am the head and not the tail. I am a beautiful colorful butterfly that now knows how to spread my wings and fly.* The sky is now her limit, so look out world because here she comes.

Through the ups and downs, heartaches and pains, she still stands. Although it took some time to realize it, she now knows that this love she was searching for has been with her the whole time. Just when she thought that there was no one else to turn to, or no one to love her, the way she always dreamt of being loved, Reba looked into her own heart. In doing so, she realized that she was never alone; all she had to do was call on the LORD OUR FATHER. For he will never leave nor forsake you.

Ladies, we are all butterflies, just waiting to spread those wings and fly. Read the story of Reba and realize that we are never alone. Many of us may go through stormy weather and they may not all be the same, but with strong faith, we are still standing. It's not always going to be easy to let go and not look back. However, just know that GOD is who he says he is.

There were times when Reba thought only if she had waited on the Lord. It wasn't long before she realized, he is truly an on time God. He sees your situation and will only allow you to go through what you can bear. In times of darkness, fall on your knees, begin to call his name, and you will surely find your light. Trust me, when he shows up, he is bound to show out.

Will there ever be a perfect life? No, but even Reba knows how to stay on the right path now. You see she now walks by faith and not by sight. In life that's all we can do.

www.ingramcontent.com/pod-product-compliance
Lightning Source LLC
Chambersburg PA
CBHW041615220426
43670CB00004B/56